The Books of Maccabees
Containing the Books of 1, 2, 3, and 4 Maccabees

Compiled by
Joseph Lumpkin

The Books of Maccabees
Containing the Books of 1, 2, 3, and 4 Maccabees

Compiled by
Joseph Lumpkin

Cover taken from the work of Sir Peter Paul Rubens (28 June 1577 - 30 May 1640)

ISBN: 9781936533701

First time or interested authors, contact Fifth Estate Publishers,

Blountsville, AL 35031.

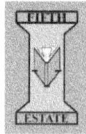

Fifth Estate, 2019

Joseph Lumpkin

Table of Contents

Joseph Lumpkin

Introduction:
A Brief History of the Apocrypha and the Books of the Maccabees

The official editions of the King James contained the books of the Apocrypha until 1796. Most printers did not clear inventories and change to the sixty-six book version we know today until the mid 1800's. Thus, most Bibles printed before 1840 still had the Apocrypha, or at least most of the Apocrypha. As it turns out, various religions have differing versions of the Bible, made up of divergent lists of books. The Protestant church has its sixty-six books, the Catholics have kept most of the Apocrypha. The Eastern Orthodox Church claims three more books than the Catholics, and the Ethiopic Church has a total of eighty-one books in its Bible.

Etymologically, the word "apocrypha" means "things that are hidden," but why they were hidden is not clear. Some have suggested that the books were "hidden" from common use because they contained esoteric knowledge, too profound to be communicated to any except the initiated (compare 2 Esd 14.45-46). Others have suggested that such books were hidden due to their spurious or heretical teaching.

According to traditional usage "Apocrypha" has been the designation applied to the fifteen books, or portions of books, listed below. In many earlier editions of the Apocrypha, the Letter of Jeremiah is incorporated as the final chapter of the Book of Baruch; hence in these editions there are fourteen books.

Tobit, Judith, The Additions to the Book of Esther (contained in the Greek version of Esther), The Wisdom of Solomon, Ecclesiasticus, The Wisdom of Jesus son of Sirach, Baruch, The Letter of Jeremiah, The Prayer of Azariah, The Song of the Three Jews ,"Susanna, Bel, and the Dragon", 1 Maccabees, 2 Maccabees, 1 Esdras, The Prayer of Manasseh, and 2 Esdras.

In addition, the present expanded edition includes the following three texts that are of special interest to Eastern Orthodox readers are 3 Maccabees, 4 Maccabees, and Psalm 151.
None of these books are included in the Hebrew canon of Holy Scripture. All of them, however, with the exception of 2 Esdras, are present in copies of the Greek version of the Old Testament known as the Septuagint. The

5

The Books of Maccabees

Old Latin translations of the Old Testament, made from the Septuagint, also include them, along with 2 Esdras. The Eastern Orthodox Churches chose to include 1 Esdras, Psalm 151, the Prayer of Manasseh, and 3 Maccabees, and 4 Maccabees, which is placed in an appendix as a historical work.

At the end of the fourth century, Pope Damasus commissioned Jerome to prepare a standard Latin version of the Scriptures called the Latin Vulgate. Jerome wrote a note or preface, designating a separate category for the apocryphal books. However, copyists failed the include Jerome's prefaces. Thus, during the medieval period the Western Church generally regarded these books as part of the holy Scriptures.

In 1546 the Council of Trent decreed that the canon of the Old Testament includes the Apocrypha with the exception of the Prayer of Manasseh and 1 and 2 Esdras. Later, the church completed the decision by writing in its Roman Catholic Catechism, "Deuterocanonical does not mean Apocryphal, but simply 'later added to the canon.'"

But wait, there's more.
The canon of the Ethiopic church contains the following Old Testament books:

Genesis
Exodus
Leviticus
Numbers
Deuteronomy
Enoch
Jubilees
Joshua
Judges
Ruth
1 Samuel
2 Samuel
1 Kings
2 Kings
1 Chronicles
2 Chronicles
Ezra
Nehemiah
3rd Ezra
4rth Ezra
Tobit
Judith

Esther (includes additions to Esther)
1 Macabees
2 Macabees
3 Macabees
Job
Psalms (+ Psalm 151)
Proverbs (Proverbs 1-24)
Täagsas (Proverbs 25-31)
Wisdom of Solomon
Ecclesiastes
Song of Solomon
Sirach (Ecclesiasticus)
Isaiah
Jeremiah
Baruch (includes Letter of Jeremiah)
Lamentations
Ezekiel
Daniel
Hosea
Amos
Micah
Joel
Obadiah
Jonah
Nahum
Habakkuk
Zephaniah
Haggai
Zecariah
Malachi

The Ethiopic Church also adds Clements and the Shepherd of Hermas to its New Testament canon. As stated before, the largest canon belongs to the Ethiopic Church or Tewahedo Church, which is a part of a set of Oriental Orthodox churches. The position of Eastern and Oriental Orthodox Churches tend to have a more flexible canon of the Old Testament, and at times the list is not at all clear. For example, the Ethiopic Church has what is called a Narrow and Broad Canon.

One list of books in the Canon gives 46 as the total for the books of the Old Testament, made up as follows: - Octateuch (8), Judith (1), Samuel and Kings (4), Chronicles (2), 1 Esdras and the Ezra Apocalypse (2), Esther (1), Tobit (1), Maccabees (2), Job (1), Psalms (1), books of Solomon (5), Prophets

(16), Ecclesiasticus (1), Pseudo-Josephus (1); Jubilees and Enoch are to be included in the number (by counting Samuel and Kings as only 2 books).

The New Testament has 35 books consisting of the Gospels (4), Acts (1), the Catholic or general epistles (7), the Pauline epistles (14), Revelation (1), Sinodos (4 sections), the Book of the Covenant (2 sections), Clement (1), Didascalia (1).

The list of books in a larger Canon is made up of the Prayers of the Church and the list of the books actually printed in the large Geez and Amharic diglot, and Amharic Bibles, issued by the Emperor's command. In this, the universally accepted 39 Old Testament books are counted as 40 by the separation of Messale (Prov. 1-24) and Tägsas (Prov. 25-31), and then 14 further books are listed as equally fully canonical, namely Enoch, Jubilees, Wisdom, 1 Esdras, Ezra Apocalypse, Judith, Tobit, Ecclesiasticus, Baruch, 'the rest of Jeremiah', book of Susanna, 'the remainder of Daniel', 1 and 2 Maccabees. This brings the Old Testament total to 54, which together with the universally accepted 27 Old Testament books makes a total of 81.

The position of the Russian Orthodox Church as regards the Apocrypha appears to have changed during the centuries. The Holy Synod ruling from St. Petersburg were in sympathy with the position of the Reformers and decided to exclude the Apocrypha and since similar influences were emanating from the universities of Kiev, Moscow, Petersburg, and Kazan, the Russian Church became united in its rejection of the Apocrypha.

This work will focus on the Books of the Maccabees. There are up to eight books that carry such a name but only four books are usually referred to as such. Of the four books of the Maccabees, three appear in the recognized canon of the Ethiopic or Tewahedo Churches, with the fourth one held as more of a historical document, held as canon only in the Georgian Orthodox Church.

The Georgian Apostolic Autocephalous Orthodox Church is an Eastern Orthodox Church, having its own leadership but still in full communion with the other churches of Eastern Orthodoxy. The Georgian Orthodox Church is one of the oldest churches in the world. It asserts apostolic foundation, and traces its roots back to the early Christianization of Iberia and Colchis by Saint Andrew in the 1st century AD and by Saint Nino in the 4th century AD, respectively. Thus, the inclusion of the Fourth Book of the Maccabees in such an ancient tradition should serve to enforce the theological and historical weight of the book.

The term, Books of the Maccabees, mostly refers to two deuterocanonical books contained in various canons of the Bible, and two lesser-known works. 1 and 2 Maccabees appear in the standard Apocrypha of the Roman catholic Bible, as well as the Bible of several Orthodox Christian canons.

1 Maccabees, originally written in Hebrew and surviving in a Greek translation, relates the history of the Maccabees from 175 BCE until 134 BCE.
2 Maccabees, a Greek abridgment of an earlier history in Hebrew, relates the history of the Maccabees down to 161 BCE, focusing on Judas Maccabaeus, discussing praying for the dead and offerings.

The term also commonly refers to two further works. 3 Maccabees appears in the Ethiopic Christian Bible.

3 Maccabees, a Greek book relating to a 3rd-century BCE persecution of the Jews of Egypt.
4 Maccabees, a philosophic discourse praising the supremacy of reason over passion, using the Maccabean martyrs as examples.

The books of 3 and 4 Maccabees are ancient Jewish writings included in various lists of the Orthodox Church canon. The canon of Orthodox deuterocanonical books and the Armenian Bible list 3 Maccabees, while 4 Maccabees is listed in the canon of the Georgian Orthodox Bible.

The book of 3 Maccabees tells the story of persecution of the Jews under Ptolemy IV Philopator (222–205 BC) . This was before the Maccabean uprising. Various scholars have dated the writing of 3 Maccabees as sometime between 100 BC and AD 30. The book does not contain information on the Maccabees, contrary to what the title implies.

The book of 4 Maccabees is a philosophic text, which argues that when results are sought, reason is superior to passion. Points are illustrated using examples drawn from the Maccabees and the martyrdom of Eleazer under Antiochus IV Epiphanes.

The early church historian Eusebius attributed 4 Maccabees to the Jewish historian Josephus. However, many critics have since disputed Josephus' authorship, though scholars generally agree 4 Maccabees was written before the fall of Jerusalem in AD 70.

The books of 1 and 2 Maccabees are early Jewish writings in the first century BC. Both books are part of the canon of Scripture in the Greek

The Books of Maccabees

Orthodox, Roman Catholic, Coptic, and Russian Orthodox churches, but they are not recognized as canon by Protestants and Jews. The books recount the history of the Maccabees, which were a family of Jewish leaders who led a rebellion of the Jews against the Seleucid Dynasty from 175 BC to 134 BC. The book of 1 Maccabees tells the story of the uprising of the Jews to regain their cultural and religious independence from Antiochus IV Epiphanes after his desecration of the Jewish temple.

The book of 2 Maccabees is more theological in its tone, and contains several doctrines followed by the Orthodox and Roman Catholic churches to this day. The book of 1 Maccabees was written in Hebrew and later translated into Greek. Scholars believe that the author was a Palestinian Jew who was familiar with the events of the Jewish revolutionaries led by Judas Maccabeus and his brothers.

The Maccabees were the leaders of the Jewish rebellion against the Seleucid dynasty and related subjects. It does not appear the name, Maccabee, was the true name of the family, but a nickname given during the revolt. In a rural village called Modein, there was an elderly priest named Mattathias, who had five sons — John, Simon, Judas, Eleazer, and Jonathan. They seemed to have first been referred to by the name, Hasmoneans, which came from Asmoneus, the name of one of their ancestors. The father was a firebrand – an outspoken and forceful family leader, who raised strong-willed sons. Thus, the family more frequently called the Maccabeans, which meaning - "hammerer". The nickname, Hammer, was further proclaimed as the armies, guided by the family "hammered away" at the Roman forces.

In 167 BC Antiochus sent his soldiers to the village of Modein to compel the Jews there to make sacrifices to the pagan gods. Mattathias, as a leader in the city, was commanded by the officers to be the first person to offer a sacrifice as an example to the rest of the people. He refused and responded by giving a powerful speech, which is written in 1 Maccabees 2:15-22. It was this speech that began the Jewish revolt. Mattathias died in 166 BC, just as the revolt was gaining momentum, leaving his son Judas in charge of the rebel forces.

1 Maccabees
Although the book presents the Jewish leaders Judas, Jonathan, and Simon as devout people and has little sympathy for people who favor

hellenization, but it must be noted that he nowhere mentions divine intervention.

The contents of the book can be summarized as follows:

Chapter 1-2: The hellenization of Judah and the non-violent resistance by Mattathias;

Chapter 3-9: Military actions by Judas the Maccabaean ('battle hammer'): after 166, he defeats the Seleucid armies three times and liberates Jerusalem, where the temple is purified; more operations; Judas' defeat and death in 161;

Chapter 9-12: Continued warfare, led by Judas' brother Jonathan (160-143), who, benefiting from wars of succession in the Seleucid Empire, restores the fortunes of the Jewish nationalists and adds to their territories;

Chapter 13-16: The third brother, Simon, achieves political independence, and founds the Hasmonaean dynasty.

The author must have been a cultivated Jew living in Judah, and can be dated to c.100 B.C.E. Although we assume there is a Hebrew or Aramaic original, which is now lost. The Greek version has survived and was accepted as canonical by the Christians. It must have been popular in the Diaspora also. In the sixteenth century, the scholars of the Reformation preferred to concentrate on those texts of the Jewish Bible that were written in Hebrew. It was at this time that the final decision was made by church fathers that if a book was not written in Hebrew it would not be considered canon for the Old Testament.

2 Maccabees

2 Maccabees has a much greater interest in theology than I Maccabees. 2 Maccabees is not as well written and has a less polished form. The pagans are defined as 'blasphemous and barbarous nations' in 10.4, but there are also severe censures of apostate Jews, of whom there must therefore have been considerable numbers. We find a theological features in 2 Maccabees such as the resurrection of the body in 7.11; 14.46. This stand in stark contrast first to Wisdom and Philo, both of which teach the immortality of the soul. In 7.28 there appears for the first time in Hebrew thought the doctrine which will later be called creatio ex nihilo, which is the belief that creation, and thus all things created, was brought about out of nothing. That is to say that God made the world not from things which were, which is not identical with 'nothing' in the philosophical sense of the term. In 7.9, 14 (cf. 14.46; 12.43) we have concepts of eternal life and death, and in 12.43 the intercession of the living for the dead, an element on which the Catholic church has sometimes sought to found the doctrine of Purgatory. Lastly, there is a well-developed angelology (3.24-28; 5.2-4; 10.29ff.; 11.8, etc.) Indeed, 2 Maccabees influenced the theology of certain churches more than any apocryphal book.

3 Maccabees
The title of 3 Maccabees is a misnomer because the book has nothing to do with the Maccabees, who are never mentioned in it. The book is a story about a situation in which the Jewish people, this time in Egypt, were in danger of being annihilated by a Hellenistic monarch, who was attempting to top their religious convictions and practices. The book was composed in Greek and relates a story set in the time of Ptolemy IV Philopater (221-203 B.C.E).

4 Maccabees
4 Maccabees belongs to the Maccabees series only because it deals with the beginning of the persecution of Jews by Antiochus IV Epiphanes. It possibly was written during the reign of the emperor Caligula (C.E. 37.) The work's main religious theme is that the martyr's sufferings expunged the sins of the entire Jewish people through a type of propitiation. The Maccabees books were preserved only by the Christian church. Augustine wrote in The City of God that they were preserved for their accounts of the martyrs. This suggests that 4 Maccabees may have been the most highly regarded of the Maccabees series, although this is disputed by the fact that 3 Maccabees may have actually established the idea of Purgatory.

Now, let us examine the texts.

1 Maccabees

1Mac.1

[1] After Alexander son of Philip, the Macedonian, who came from the land of Kittim, had defeated Darius, king of the Persians and the Medes, he succeeded him as king. (He had previously become king of Greece.)

[2] He fought many battles, conquered strongholds, and put to death the kings of the earth.

[3] He advanced to the ends of the earth, and plundered many nations. When the earth became quiet before him, he was exalted, and his heart was lifted up.

[4] He gathered a very strong army and ruled over countries, nations, and princes, and they became tributary to him.

[5] After this he fell sick and perceived that he was dying.

[6] So he summoned his most honored officers, who had been brought up with him from youth, and divided his kingdom among them while he was still alive.

[7] And after Alexander had reigned twelve years, he died.

[8] Then his officers began to rule, each in his own place.

[9] They all put on crowns after his death, and so did their sons after them for many years; and they caused many evils on the earth.

[10] From them came forth a sinful root, Antiochus Epiphanes, son of Antiochus the king; he had been a hostage in Rome. He began to reign in the one hundred and thirty-seventh year of the kingdom of the Greeks.

[11] In those days lawless men came forth from Israel, and misled many, saying, "Let us go and make a covenant with the Gentiles round about us, for since we separated from them many evils have come upon us."

[12] This proposal pleased them,

[13] and some of the people eagerly went to the king. He authorized them to observe the ordinances of the Gentiles.

[14] So they built a gymnasium in Jerusalem, according to Gentile custom,

[15] and removed the marks of circumcision, and abandoned the holy covenant. They joined with the Gentiles and sold themselves to do evil.

[16] When Antiochus saw that his kingdom was established, he determined to become king of the land of Egypt, that he might reign over both kingdoms.

[17] So he invaded Egypt with a strong force, with chariots and elephants and cavalry and with a large fleet.

[18] He engaged Ptolemy king of Egypt in battle, and Ptolemy turned and fled before him, and many were wounded and fell.

[19] And they captured the fortified cities in the land of Egypt, and he plundered the land of Egypt.

[20] After subduing Egypt, Antiochus returned in the one hundred and forty-third year. He went up against Israel and came to Jerusalem with a strong force.

[21] He arrogantly entered the sanctuary and took the golden altar, the lampstand for the light, and all its utensils.

[22] He took also the table for the bread of the Presence, the cups for drink offerings, the bowls, the golden censers, the curtain, the crowns, and the gold decoration on the front of the temple; he stripped it all off.

[23] He took the silver and the gold, and the costly vessels; he took also the hidden treasures which he found.

[24] Taking them all, he departed to his own land. He committed deeds of murder, and spoke with great arrogance.

[25] Israel mourned deeply in every community,

[26] rulers and elders groaned, maidens and young men became faint, the beauty of women faded.

[27] Every bridegroom took up the lament; she who sat in the bridal chamber was mourning.

[28] Even the land shook for its inhabitants, and all the house of Jacob was clothed with shame.

[29] Two years later the king sent to the cities of Judah a chief collector of tribute, and he came to Jerusalem with a large force.

[30] Deceitfully he spoke peaceable words to them, and they believed him; but he suddenly fell upon the city, dealt it a severe blow, and destroyed many people of Israel.

[31] He plundered the city, burned it with fire, and tore down its houses and its surrounding walls.

[32] And they took captive the women and children, and seized the cattle.

[33] Then they fortified the city of David with a great strong wall and strong towers, and it became their citadel.

[34] And they stationed there a sinful people, lawless men. These strengthened their position;

[35] they stored up arms and food, and collecting the spoils of Jerusalem they stored them there, and became a great snare.

[36] It became an ambush against the sanctuary, an evil adversary of Israel continually.

[37] On every side of the sanctuary they shed innocent blood; they even defiled the sanctuary.

[38] Because of them the residents of Jerusalem fled; she became a dwelling of strangers; she became strange to her offspring, and her children forsook her.

[39] Her sanctuary became desolate as a desert; her feasts were turned into mourning, her sabbaths into a reproach,

her honor into contempt.

[40] Her dishonor now grew as great as her glory; her exaltation was turned into mourning.

[41] Then the king wrote to his whole kingdom that all should be one people,

[42] and that each should give up his customs.

[43] All the Gentiles accepted the command of the king. Many even from Israel gladly adopted his religion; they sacrificed to idols and profaned the sabbath.

[44] And the king sent letters by messengers to Jerusalem and the cities of Judah; he directed them to follow customs strange to the land,

[45] to forbid burnt offerings and sacrifices and drink offerings in the sanctuary, to profane sabbaths and feasts,

[46] to defile the sanctuary and the priests,

[47] to build altars and sacred precincts and shrines for idols, to sacrifice swine and unclean animals,

[48] and to leave their sons uncircumcised. They were to make themselves abominable by everything unclean and profane,

[49] so that they should forget the law and change all the ordinances.

[50] "And whoever does not obey the command of the king shall die."

[51] In such words he wrote to his whole kingdom. And he appointed inspectors over all the people and commanded the cities of Judah to offer sacrifice, city by city.

[52] Many of the people, every one who forsook the law, joined them, and they did evil in the land;

[53] they drove Israel into hiding in every place of refuge they had.

[54] Now on the fifteenth day of Chislev, in the one hundred and forty-fifth year, they erected a desolating sacrilege upon the altar of burnt offering. They also built altars in the surrounding cities of Judah,

[55] and burned incense at the doors of the houses and in the streets.

[56] The books of the law which they found they tore to pieces and burned with fire.

[57] Where the book of the covenant was found in the possession of any one, or if any one adhered to the law, the decree of the king condemned him to death.

[58] They kept using violence against Israel, against those found month after month in the cities.

[59] And on the twenty-fifth day of the month they offered sacrifice on the altar which was upon the altar of burnt offering.

[60] According to the decree, they put to death the women who had their children circumcised,

[61] and their families and those who circumcised them; and they hung the infants from their mothers' necks.

[62] But many in Israel stood firm and were resolved in their hearts not to eat unclean food.

[63] They chose to die rather than to be defiled by food or to profane the holy covenant; and they did die.

[64] And very great wrath came upon Israel.

1Mac.2

[1] In those days Mattathias the son of John, son of Simeon, a priest of the sons of Joarib, moved from Jerusalem and settled in Modein.

[2] He had five sons, John surnamed Gaddi,

[3] Simon called Thassi,

[4] Judas called Maccabeus,

[5] Eleazar called Avaran, and Jonathan called Apphus.

[6] He saw the blasphemies being committed in Judah and Jerusalem,

[7] and said, "Alas! Why was I born to see this, the ruin of my people, the ruin of the holy city, and to dwell there when it was given over to the enemy, the sanctuary given over to aliens?

[8] Her temple has become like a man without honor;

[9] her glorious vessels have been carried into captivity. Her babes have been killed in her streets, her youths by the sword of the foe.

[10] What nation has not inherited her palaces and has not seized her spoils?

[11] All her adornment has been taken away; no longer free, she has become a slave.

[12] And behold, our holy place, our beauty, and our glory have been laid waste; the Gentiles have profaned it.

[13] Why should we live any longer?"

[14] And Mattathias and his sons rent their clothes, put on sackcloth, and mourned greatly.

[15] Then the king's officers who were enforcing the apostasy came to the city of Modein to make them offer sacrifice.

[16] Many from Israel came to them; and Mattathias and his sons were assembled.

[17] Then the king's officers spoke to Mattathias as follows: "You are a leader, honored and great in this city, and supported by sons and brothers.

[18] Now be the first to come and do what the king commands, as all the Gentiles and the men of Judah and those that are left in Jerusalem have done. Then you and your sons will be numbered among the friends of the king, and you and your sons will be honored with silver and gold and many gifts."

[19] But Mattathias answered and said in a loud voice: "Even if all the nations that live under the rule of the king obey him, and have chosen to do his commandments, departing each one from the religion of his fathers,

[20] yet I and my sons and my brothers will live by the covenant of our fathers.

[21] Far be it from us to desert the law and the ordinances.

[22] We will not obey the king's words by turning aside from our religion to the right hand or to the left."

[23] When he had finished speaking these words, a Jew came forward in the sight of all to offer sacrifice upon the altar in Modein, according to the king's command.

[24] When Mattathias saw it, be burned with zeal and his heart was stirred. He gave vent to righteous anger; he ran and killed him upon the altar.

[25] At the same time he killed the king's officer who was forcing them to sacrifice, and he tore down the altar.

[26] Thus he burned with zeal for the law, as Phinehas did against Zimri the son of Salu.

[27] Then Mattathias cried out in the city with a loud voice, saying: "Let every one who is zealous for the law and supports the covenant come out with me!"

[28] And he and his sons fled to the hills and left all that they had in the city.

[29] Then many who were seeking righteousness and justice went down to the wilderness to dwell there,

[30] they, their sons, their wives, and their cattle, because evils pressed heavily upon them.

[31] And it was reported to the king's officers, and to the troops in Jerusalem the city of David, that men who had rejected the king's command had gone down to the hiding places in the wilderness.

[32] Many pursued them, and overtook them; they encamped opposite them and prepared for battle against them on the sabbath day.

[33] And they said to them, "Enough of this! Come out and do what the king commands, and you will live."

[34] But they said, "We will not come out, nor will we do what the king commands and so profane the sabbath day."

[35] Then the enemy hastened to attack them.

[36] But they did not answer them or hurl a stone at them or block up their hiding places,

[37] for they said, "Let us all die in our innocence; heaven and earth testify for us that you are killing us unjustly."

[38] So they attacked them on the sabbath, and they died, with their wives and children and cattle, to the number of a thousand persons.

[39] When Mattathias and his friends learned of it, they mourned for them deeply.

[40] And each said to his neighbor: "If we all do as our brethren have done and refuse to fight with the Gentiles for our lives and for our ordinances, they will quickly destroy us from the earth."

[41] So they made this decision that day: "Let us fight against every man who comes to attack us on the sabbath day; let us not all die as our brethren died in their hiding places."

[42] Then there united with them a company of Hasideans, mighty warriors of Israel, every one who offered himself willingly for the law.

[43] And all who became fugitives to escape their troubles joined them and reinforced them.

[44] They organized an army, and struck down sinners in their anger and lawless men in their wrath; the survivors fled to the Gentiles for safety.

[45] And Mattathias and his friends went about and tore down the altars;

[46] they forcibly circumcised all the uncircumcised boys that they found within the borders of Israel.

[47] They hunted down the arrogant men, and the work prospered in their hands.

[48] They rescued the law out of the hands of the Gentiles and kings, and they never let the sinner gain the upper hand.

[49] Now the days drew near for Mattathias to die, and he said to his sons: "Arrogance and reproach have now become strong; it is a time of ruin and furious anger.

[50] Now, my children, show zeal for the law, and give your lives for the covenant of our fathers.

[51] "Remember the deeds of the fathers, which they did in their generations; and receive great honor and an everlasting name.

[52] Was not Abraham found faithful when tested, and it was reckoned to him as righteousness?

[53] Joseph in the time of his distress kept the commandment, and became lord of Egypt.

[54] Phinehas our father, because he was deeply zealous, received the covenant of everlasting priesthood.

[55] Joshua, because he fulfilled the command, became a judge in Israel.

[56] Caleb, because he testified in the assembly, received an inheritance in the land.

[57] David, because he was merciful, inherited the throne of the kingdom for ever.

[58] Elijah because of great zeal for the law was taken up into heaven.

[59] Hannaniah, Azariah, and Mishael believed and were saved from the flame.

[60] Daniel because of his innocence was delivered from the mouth of the lions.

[61] "And so observe, from generation to generation, that none who put their trust in him will lack strength.

[62] Do not fear the words of a sinner, for his splendor will turn into dung and worms.

[63] Today he will be exalted, but tomorrow he will not be found, because he has returned to the dust, and his plans will perish.

[64] My children, be courageous and grow strong in the law, for by it you will gain honor.

[65] "Now behold, I know that Simeon your brother is wise in counsel; always listen to him; he shall be your father.

[66] Judas Maccabeus has been a mighty warrior from his youth; he shall command the army for you and fight the battle against the peoples.

[67] You shall rally about you all who observe the law, and avenge the wrong done to your people.

[68] Pay back the Gentiles in full, and heed what the law commands."

[69] Then he blessed them, and was gathered to his fathers.

[70] He died in the one hundred and forty-sixth year and was buried in the tomb of his fathers at Modein. And all Israel mourned for him with great lamentation.

1Mac.3

[1] Then Judas his son, who was called Maccabeus, took command in his place.

[2] All his brothers and all who had joined his father helped him; they gladly fought for Israel.

[3] He extended the glory of his people. Like a giant he put on his breastplate; he girded on his armor of war and waged battles, protecting the host by his sword.

[4] He was like a lion in his deeds, like a lion's cub roaring for prey.

[5] He searched out and pursued the lawless; he burned those who troubled his people.

[6] Lawless men shrank back for fear of him; all the evildoers were confounded; and deliverance prospered by his hand.

[7] He embittered many kings, but he made Jacob glad by his deeds, and his memory is blessed for ever.

[8] He went through the cities of Judah; he destroyed the ungodly out of the land; thus he turned away wrath from Israel.

[9] He was renowned to the ends of the earth; he gathered in those who were perishing.

[10] But Apollonius gathered together Gentiles and a large force from Samaria to fight against Israel.

[11] When Judas learned of it, he went out to meet him, and he defeated and killed him. Many were wounded and fell, and the rest fled.

[12] Then they seized their spoils; and Judas took the sword of Apollonius, and used it in battle the rest of his life.

[13] Now when Seron, the commander of the Syrian army, heard that Judas had gathered a large company, including a body of faithful men who stayed with him and went out to battle,

[14] he said, "I will make a name for myself and win honor in the kingdom. I will make war on Judas and his companions, who scorn the king's command."

[15] And again a strong army of ungodly men went up with him to help him, to take vengeance on the sons of Israel.

[16] When he approached the ascent of Beth-horon, Judas went out to meet him with a small company.

[17] But when they saw the army coming to meet them, they said to Judas, "How can we, few as we are, fight against so great and strong a multitude? And we are faint, for we have eaten nothing today."

[18] Judas replied, "It is easy for many to be hemmed in by few, for in the sight of Heaven there is no difference between saving by many or by few.

[19] It is not on the size of the army that victory in battle depends, but strength comes from Heaven.

[20] They come against us in great pride and lawlessness to destroy us and our wives and our children, and to despoil us;

[21] but we fight for our lives and our laws.

[22] He himself will crush them before us; as for you, do not be afraid of them."

[23] When he finished speaking, he rushed suddenly against Seron and his army, and they were crushed before him.

[24] They pursued them down the descent of Beth-horon to the plain; eight hundred of them fell, and the rest fled into the land of the Philistines.

[25] Then Judas and his brothers began to be feared, and terror fell upon the Gentiles round about them.

[26] His fame reached the king, and the Gentiles talked of the battles of Judas.

[27] When king Antiochus heard these reports, he was greatly angered; and he sent and gathered all the forces of his kingdom, a very strong army.

[28] And he opened his coffers and gave a year's pay to his forces, and ordered them to be ready for any need.

[29] Then he saw that the money in the treasury was exhausted, and that the revenues from the country were small because of the dissension and disaster which he had caused in the land by abolishing the laws that had existed from the earliest days.

[30] He feared that he might not have such funds as he had before for his expenses and for the gifts which he used to give more lavishly than preceding kings.

[31] He was greatly perplexed in mind, and determined to go to Persia and collect the revenues from those regions and raise a large fund.

[32] He left Lysias, a distinguished man of royal lineage, in charge of the king's affairs from the river Euphrates to the borders of Egypt.

[33] Lysias was also to take care of Antiochus his son until he returned.

[34] And he turned over to Lysias half of his troops and the elephants, and gave him orders about all that he wanted done. As for the residents of Judea and Jerusalem,
[35] Lysias was to send a force against them to wipe out and destroy the strength of Israel and the remnant of Jerusalem; he was to banish the memory of them from the place,
[36] settle aliens in all their territory, and distribute their land.
[37] Then the king took the remaining half of his troops and departed from Antioch his capital in the one hundred and forty-seventh year. He crossed the Euphrates river and went through the upper provinces.
[38] Lysias chose Ptolemy the son of Dorymenes, and Nicanor and Gorgias, mighty men among the friends of the king,
[39] and sent with them forty thousand infantry and seven thousand cavalry to go into the land of Judah and destroy it, as the king had commanded.
[40] so they departed with their entire force, and when they arrived they encamped near Emmaus in the plain.
[41] When the traders of the region heard what was said to them, they took silver and gold in immense amounts, and fetters, and went to the camp to get the sons of Israel for slaves. And forces from Syria and the land of the Philistines joined with them.
[42] Now Judas and his brothers saw that misfortunes had increased and that the forces were encamped in their territory. They also learned what the king had commanded to do to the people to cause their final destruction.
[43] But they said to one another, "Let us repair the destruction of our people, and fight for our people and the sanctuary."
[44] And the congregation assembled to be ready for battle, and to pray and ask for mercy and compassion.
[45] Jerusalem was uninhabited like a wilderness; not one of her children went in or out.The sanctuary was trampled own,
and the sons of aliens held the citadel; it was a lodging place for the Gentiles. Joy was taken from Jacob; the flute and the harp ceased to play.
[46] So they assembled and went to Mizpah, opposite Jerusalem, because Israel formerly had a place of prayer in Mizpah.
[47] They fasted that day, put on sackcloth and sprinkled ashes on their heads, and rent their clothes.
[48] And they opened the book of the law to inquire into those matters about which the Gentiles were consulting the images of their idols.
[49] They also brought the garments of the priesthood and the first fruits and the tithes, and they stirred up the Nazirites who had completed their days;
[50] and they cried aloud to Heaven, saying, "What shall we do with these? Where shall we take them?

[51] Your sanctuary is trampled down and profaned, and thy priests mourn in humiliation.

[52] And behold, the Gentiles are assembled against us to destroy us; thou knowest what they plot against us.

[53] How will we be able to withstand them, if thou do not help us?"

[54] Then they sounded the trumpets and gave a loud shout.

[55] After this Judas appointed leaders of the people, in charge of thousands and hundreds and fifties and tens.

[56] And he said to those who were building houses, or were betrothed, or were planting vineyards, or were fainthearted, that each should return to his home, according to the law.

[57] Then the army marched out and encamped to the south of Emmaus.

[58] And Judas said, "Gird yourselves and be valiant. Be ready early in the morning to fight with these Gentiles who have assembled against us to destroy us and our sanctuary.

[59] It is better for us to die in battle than to see the misfortunes of our nation and of the sanctuary.

[60] But as his will in heaven may be, so he will do."

1Mac.4

[1] Now Gorgias took five thousand infantry and a thousand picked cavalry, and this division moved out by night

[2] to fall upon the camp of the Jews and attack them suddenly. Men from the citadel were his guides.

[3] But Judas heard of it, and he and his mighty men moved out to attack the king's force in Emmaus

[4] while the division was still absent from the camp.

[5] When Gorgias entered the camp of Judas by night, he found no one there, so he looked for them in the hills, because he said, "These men are fleeing from us."

[6] At daybreak Judas appeared in the plain with three thousand men, but they did not have armor and swords such as they desired.

[7] And they saw the camp of the Gentiles, strong and fortified, with cavalry round about it; and these men were trained in war.

[8] But Judas said to the men who were with him, "Do not fear their numbers or be afraid when they charge.

[9] Remember how our fathers were saved at the Red Sea, when Pharaoh with his forces pursued them.

[10] And now let us cry to Heaven, to see whether he will favor us and remember his covenant with our fathers and crush this army before us today.

[11] Then all the Gentiles will know that there is one who redeems and saves Israel."

[12] When the foreigners looked up and saw them coming against them,

[13] they went forth from their camp to battle. Then the men with Judas blew their trumpets
[14] and engaged in battle. The Gentiles were crushed and fled into the plain,
[15] and all those in the rear fell by the sword. They pursued them to Gazara, and to the plains of Idumea, and to Azotus and Jamnia; and three thousand of them fell.
[16] Then Judas and his force turned back from pursuing them,
[17] and he said to the people, "Do not be greedy for plunder, for there is a battle before us;
[18] Gorgias and his force are near us in the hills. But stand now against our enemies and fight them, and afterward seize the plunder boldly."
[19] Just as Judas was finishing this speech, a detachment appeared, coming out of the hills.
[20] They saw that their army had been put to flight, and that the Jews were burning the camp, for the smoke that was seen showed what had happened.
[21] When they perceived this they were greatly frightened, and when they also saw the army of Judas drawn up in the plain for battle,
[22] they all fled into the land of the Philistines.
[23] Then Judas returned to plunder the camp, and they seized much gold and silver, and cloth dyed blue and sea purple, and great riches.
[24] On their return they sang hymns and praises to Heaven, for he is good, for his mercy endures for ever.
[25] Thus Israel had a great deliverance that day.
[26] Those of the foreigners who escaped went and reported to Lysias all that had happened.
[27] When he heard it, he was perplexed and discouraged, for things had not happened to Israel as he had intended, nor had they turned out as the king had commanded him.
[28] But the next year he mustered sixty thousand picked infantrymen and five thousand cavalry to subdue them.
[29] They came into Idumea and encamped at Beth-zur, and Judas met them with ten thousand men.
[30] When he saw that the army was strong, he prayed, saying, "Blessed art thou, O Savior of Israel, who didst crush the attack of the mighty warrior by the hand of thy servant David, and didst give the camp of the Philistines into the hands of Jonathan, the son of Saul, and of the man who carried his armor.
[31] So do thou hem in this army by the hand of thy people Israel, and let them be ashamed of their troops and their cavalry.
[32] Fill them with cowardice; melt the boldness of their strength; let them tremble in their destruction.

[33] Strike them down with the sword of those who love thee, and let all who know thy name praise thee with hymns."

[34] Then both sides attacked, and there fell of the army of Lysias five thousand men; they fell in action.

[35] And when Lysias saw the rout of his troops and observed the boldness which inspired those of Judas, and how ready they were either to live or to die nobly, he departed to Antioch and enlisted mercenaries, to invade Judea again with an even larger army.

[36] Then said Judas and his brothers, "Behold, our enemies are crushed; let us go up to cleanse the sanctuary and dedicate it."

[37] So all the army assembled and they went up to Mount Zion.

[38] And they saw the sanctuary desolate, the altar profaned, and the gates burned. In the courts they saw bushes sprung up as in a thicket, or as on one of the mountains. They saw also the chambers of the priests in ruins.

[39] Then they rent their clothes, and mourned with great lamentation, and sprinkled themselves with ashes.

[40] They fell face down on the ground, and sounded the signal on the trumpets, and cried out to Heaven.

[41] Then Judas detailed men to fight against those in the citadel until he had cleansed the sanctuary.

[42] He chose blameless priests devoted to the law,

[43] and they cleansed the sanctuary and removed the defiled stones to an unclean place.

[44] They deliberated what to do about the altar of burnt offering, which had been profaned.

[45] And they thought it best to tear it down, lest it bring reproach upon them, for the Gentiles had defiled it. So they tore down the altar,

[46] and stored the stones in a convenient place on the temple hill until there should come a prophet to tell what to do with them.

[47] Then they took unhewn stones, as the law directs, and built a new altar like the former one.

[48] They also rebuilt the sanctuary and the interior of the temple, and consecrated the courts.

[49] They made new holy vessels, and brought the lampstand, the altar of incense, and the table into the temple.

[50] Then they burned incense on the altar and lighted the lamps on the lampstand, and these gave light in the temple.

[51] They placed the bread on the table and hung up the curtains. Thus they finished all the work they had undertaken.

[52] Early in the morning on the twenty-fifth day of the ninth month, which is the month of Chislev, in the one hundred and forty-eighth year,

[53] they rose and offered sacrifice, as the law directs, on the new altar of burnt offering which they had built.

[54] At the very season and on the very day that the Gentiles had profaned it, it was dedicated with songs and harps and lutes and cymbals.
[55] All the people fell on their faces and worshiped and blessed Heaven, who had prospered them.
[56] So they celebrated the dedication of the altar for eight days, and offered burnt offerings with gladness; they offered a sacrifice of deliverance and praise.
[57] They decorated the front of the temple with golden crowns and small shields; they restored the gates and the chambers for the priests, and furnished them with doors.
[58] There was very great gladness among the people, and the reproach of the Gentiles was removed.
[59] Then Judas and his brothers and all the assembly of Israel determined that every year at that season the days of dedication of the altar should be observed with gladness and joy for eight days, beginning with the twenty-fifth day of the month of Chislev.
[60] At that time they fortified Mount Zion with high walls and strong towers round about, to keep the Gentiles from coming and trampling them down as they had done before.
[61] And he stationed a garrison there to hold it. He also fortified Beth-zur, so that the people might have a stronghold that faced Idumea.
1Mac.5
[1] When the Gentiles round about heard that the altar had been built and the sanctuary dedicated as it was before, they became very angry,
[2] and they determined to destroy the descendants of Jacob who lived among them. So they began to kill and destroy among the people.
[3] But Judas made war on the sons of Esau in Idumea, at Akrabattene, because they kept lying in wait for Israel. He dealt them a heavy blow and humbled them and despoiled them.
[4] He also remembered the wickedness of the sons of Baean, who were a trap and a snare to the people and ambushed them on the highways.
[5] They were shut up by him in their towers; and he encamped against them, vowed their complete destruction, and burned with fire their towers and all who were in them.
[6] Then he crossed over to attack the Ammonites, where he found a strong band and many people with Timothy as their leader.
[7] He engaged in many battles with them and they were crushed before him; he struck them down.
[8] He also took Jazer and its villages; then he returned to Judea.
[9] Now the Gentiles in Gilead gathered together against the Israelites who lived in their territory, and planned to destroy them. But they fled to the stronghold of Dathema,
[10] and sent to Judas and his brothers a letter which said, "The Gentiles around us have gathered together against us to destroy us.

[11] They are preparing to come and capture the stronghold to which we have fled, and Timothy is leading their forces.

[12] Now then come and rescue us from their hands, for many of us have fallen,

[13] and all our brethren who were in the land of Tob have been killed; the enemy have captured their wives and children and goods, and have destroyed about a thousand men there."

[14] While the letter was still being read, behold, other messengers, with their garments rent, came from Galilee and made a similar report;

[15] they said that against them had gathered together men of Ptolemais and Tyre and Sidon, and all Galilee of the Gentiles, "to annihilate us."

[16] When Judas and the people heard these messages, a great assembly was called to determine what they should do for their brethren who were in distress and were being attacked by enemies.

[17] Then Judas said to Simon his brother, "Choose your men and go and rescue your brethren in Galilee; I and Jonathan my brother will go to Gilead."

[18] But he left Joseph, the son of Zechariah, and Azariah, a leader of the people, with the rest of the forces, in Judea to guard it;

[19] and he gave them this command, "Take charge of this people, but do not engage in battle with the Gentiles until we return."

[20] Then three thousand men were assigned to Simon to go to Galilee, and eight thousand to Judas for Gilead.

[21] so Simon went to Galilee and fought many battles against the Gentiles, and the Gentiles were crushed before him.

[22] He pursued them to the gate of Ptolemais, and as many as three thousand of the Gentiles fell, and he despoiled them.

[23] Then he took the Jews of Galilee and Arbatta, with their wives and children, and all they possessed, and led them to Judea with great rejoicing.

[24] Judas Maccabeus and Jonathan his brother crossed the Jordan and went three days' journey into the wilderness.

[25] They encountered the Nabateans, who met them peaceably and told them all that had happened to their brethren in Gilead:

[26] "Many of them have been shut up in Bozrah and Bosor, in Alema and Chaspho, Maked and Carnaim" -- all these cities were strong and large--

[27] "and some have been shut up in the other cities of Gilead; the enemy are getting ready to attack the strongholds tomorrow and take and destroy all these men in one day."

[28] Then Judas and his army quickly turned back by the wilderness road to Bozrah; and he took the city, and killed every male by the edge of the sword; then he seized all its spoils and burned it with fire.

[29] He departed from there at night, and they went all the way to the stronghold of Dathema.

[30] At dawn they looked up, and behold, a large company, that could not be counted, carrying ladders and engines of war to capture the stronghold, and attacking the Jews within.
[31] So Judas saw that the battle had begun and that the cry of the city went up to Heaven with trumpets and loud shouts,
[32] and he said to the men of his forces, "Fight today for your brethren!"
[33] Then he came up behind them in three companies, who sounded their trumpets and cried aloud in prayer.
[34] And when the army of Timothy realized that it was Maccabeus, they fled before him, and he dealt them a heavy blow. As many as eight thousand of them fell that day.
[35] Next he turned aside to Alema, and fought against it and took it; and he killed every male in it, plundered it, and burned it with fire.
[36] From there he marched on and took Chaspho, Maked, and Bosor, and the other cities of Gilead.
[37] After these things Timothy gathered another army and encamped opposite Raphon, on the other side of the stream.
[38] Judas sent men to spy out the camp, and they reported to him, "All the Gentiles around us have gathered to him; it is a very large force.
[39] They also have hired Arabs to help them, and they are encamped across the stream, ready to come and fight against you." And Judas went to meet them.
[40] Now as Judas and his army drew near to the stream of water, Timothy said to the officers of his forces, "If he crosses over to us first, we will not be able to resist him, for he will surely defeat us.
[41] But if he shows fear and camps on the other side of the river, we will cross over to him and defeat him."
[42] When Judas approached the stream of water, he stationed the scribes of the people at the stream and gave them this command, "Permit no man to encamp, but make them all enter the battle."
[43] Then he crossed over against them first, and the whole army followed him. All the Gentiles were defeated before him, and they threw away their arms and fled into the sacred precincts at Carnaim.
[44] But he took the city and burned the sacred precincts with fire, together with all who were in them. Thus Carnaim was conquered; they could stand before Judas no longer.
[45] Then Judas gathered together all the Israelites in Gilead, the small and the great, with their wives and children and goods, a very large company, to go to the land of Judah.
[46] So they came to Ephron. This was a large and very strong city on the road, and they could not go round it to the right or to the left; they had to go through it.
[47] But the men of the city shut them out and blocked up the gates with stones.

[48] And Judas sent them this friendly message, "Let us pass through your land to get to our land. No one will do you harm; we will simply pass by on foot." But they refused to open to him.

[49] Then Judas ordered proclamation to be made to the army that each should encamp where he was.

[50] So the men of the forces encamped, and he fought against the city all that day and all the night, and the city was delivered into his hands.

[51] He destroyed every male by the edge of the sword, and razed and plundered the city. Then he passed through the city over the slain.

[52] And they crossed the Jordan into the large plain before Beth-shan.

[53] And Judas kept rallying the laggards and encouraging the people all the way till he came to the land of Judah.

[54] So they went up to Mount Zion with gladness and joy, and offered burnt offerings, because not one of them had fallen before they returned in safety.

[55] Now while Judas and Jonathan were in Gilead and Simon his brother was in Galilee before Ptolemais,

[56] Joseph, the son of Zechariah, and Azariah, the commanders of the forces, heard of their brave deeds and of the heroic war they had fought.

[57] So they said, "Let us also make a name for ourselves; let us go and make war on the Gentiles around us."

[58] And they issued orders to the men of the forces that were with them, and they marched against Jamnia.

[59] And Gorgias and his men came out of the city to meet them in battle.

[60] Then Joseph and Azariah were routed, and were pursued to the borders of Judea; as many as two thousand of the people of Israel fell that day.

[61] Thus the people suffered a great rout because, thinking to do a brave deed, they did not listen to Judas and his brothers.

[62] But they did not belong to the family of those men through whom deliverance was given to Israel.

[63] The man Judas and his brothers were greatly honored in all Israel and among all the Gentiles, wherever their name was heard.

[64] Men gathered to them and praised them.

[65] Then Judas and his brothers went forth and fought the sons of Esau in the land to the south. He struck Hebron and its villages and tore down its strongholds and burned its towers round about.

[66] Then he marched off to go into the land of the Philistines, and passed through Marisa.

[67] On that day some priests, who wished to do a brave deed, fell in battle, for they went out to battle unwisely.

[68] But Judas turned aside to Azotus in the land of the Philistines; he tore down their altars, and the graven images of their gods he burned with fire; he plundered the cities and returned to the land of Judah.

1Mac.6

[1] King Antiochus was going through the upper provinces when he heard that Elymais in Persia was a city famed for its wealth in silver and gold.

[2] Its temple was very rich, containing golden shields, breastplates, and weapons left there by Alexander, the son of Philip, the Macedonian king who first reigned over the Greeks.

[3] So he came and tried to take the city and plunder it, but he could not, because his plan became known to the men of the city

[4] and they withstood him in battle. So he fled and in great grief departed from there to return to Babylon.

[5] Then some one came to him in Persia and reported that the armies which had gone into the land of Judah had been routed;

[6] that Lysias had gone first with a strong force, but had turned and fled before the Jews; that the Jews had grown strong from the arms, supplies, and abundant spoils which they had taken from the armies they had cut down;

[7] that they had torn down the abomination which he had erected upon the altar in Jerusalem; and that they had surrounded the sanctuary with high walls as before, and also Beth-zur, his city.

[8] When the king heard this news, he was astounded and badly shaken. He took to his bed and became sick from grief, because things had not turned out for him as he had planned.

[9] He lay there for many days, because deep grief continually gripped him, and he concluded that he was dying.

[10] So he called all his friends and said to them, "Sleep departs from my eyes and I am downhearted with worry.

[11] I said to myself, `To what distress I have come! And into what a great flood I now am plunged! For I was kind and beloved in my power.'

[12] But now I remember the evils I did in Jerusalem. I seized all her vessels of silver and gold; and I sent to destroy the inhabitants of Judah without good reason.

[13] I know that it is because of this that these evils have come upon me; and behold, I am perishing of deep grief in a strange land."

[14] Then he called for Philip, one of his friends, and made him ruler over all his kingdom.

[15] He gave him the crown and his robe and the signet, that he might guide Antiochus his son and bring him up to be king.

[16] Thus Antiochus the king died there in the one hundred and forty-ninth year.

[17] And when Lysias learned that the king was dead, he set up Antiochus the king's son to reign. Lysias had brought him up as a boy, and he named him Eupator.

[18] Now the men in the citadel kept hemming Israel in around the sanctuary. They were trying in every way to harm them and strengthen the Gentiles.

[19] So Judas decided to destroy them, and assembled all the people to besiege them.

[20] They gathered together and besieged the citadel in the one hundred and fiftieth year; and he built siege towers and other engines of war.

[21] But some of the garrison escaped from the siege and some of the ungodly Israelites joined them.

[22] They went to the king and said, "How long will you fail to do justice and to avenge our brethren?

[23] We were happy to serve your father, to live by what he said and to follow his commands.

[24] For this reason the sons of our people besieged the citadel and became hostile to us; moreover, they have put to death as many of us as they have caught, and they have seized our inheritances.

[25] And not against us alone have they stretched out their hands, but also against all the lands on their borders.

[26] And behold, today they have encamped against the citadel in Jerusalem to take it; they have fortified both the sanctuary and Beth-zur;

[27] and unless you quickly prevent them, they will do still greater things, and you will not be able to stop them."

[28] The king was enraged when he heard this. He assembled all his friends, the commanders of his forces and those in authority.

[29] And mercenary forces came to him from other kingdoms and from islands of the seas.

[30] The number of his forces was a hundred thousand foot soldiers, twenty thousand horsemen, and thirty-two elephants accustomed to war.

[31] They came through Idumea and encamped against Beth-zur, and for many days they fought and built engines of war; but the Jews sallied out and burned these with fire, and fought manfully.

[32] Then Judas marched away from the citadel and encamped at Beth-zechariah, opposite the camp of the king.

[33] Early in the morning the king rose and took his army by a forced march along the road to Beth-zechariah, and his troops made ready for battle and sounded their trumpets.

[34] They showed the elephants the juice of grapes and mulberries, to arouse them for battle.

[35] And they distributed the beasts among the phalanxes; with each elephant they stationed a thousand men armed with coats of mail, and with brass helmets on their heads; and five hundred picked horsemen were assigned to each beast.

[36] These took their position beforehand wherever the beast was; wherever it went they went with it, and they never left it.

[37] And upon the elephants were wooden towers, strong and covered; they were fastened upon each beast by special harness, and upon each were four armed men who fought from there, and also its Indian driver.
[38] The rest of the horsemen were stationed on either side, on the two flanks of the army, to harass the enemy while being themselves protected by the phalanxes.
[39] When the sun shone upon the shields of gold and brass, the hills were ablaze with them and gleamed like flaming torches.
[40] Now a part of the king's army was spread out on the high hills, and some troops were on the plain, and they advanced steadily and in good order.
[41] All who heard the noise made by their multitude, by the marching of the multitude and the clanking of their arms, trembled, for the army was very large and strong.
[42] But Judas and his army advanced to the battle, and six hundred men of the king's army fell.
[43] And Eleazar, called Avaran, saw that one of the beasts was equipped with royal armor. It was taller than all the others, and he supposed that the king was upon it.
[44] So he gave his life to save his people and to win for himself an everlasting name.
[45] He courageously ran into the midst of the phalanx to reach it; he killed men right and left, and they parted before him on both sides.
[46] He got under the elephant, stabbed it from beneath, and killed it; but it fell to the ground upon him and he died.
[47] And when the Jews saw the royal might and the fierce attack of the forces, they turned away in flight.
[48] The soldiers of the king's army went up to Jerusalem against them, and the king encamped in Judea and at Mount Zion.
[49] He made peace with the men of Beth-zur, and they evacuated the city, because they had no provisions there to withstand a siege, since it was a sabbatical year for the land.
[50] So the king took Beth-zur and stationed a guard there to hold it.
[51] Then he encamped before the sanctuary for many days. He set up siege towers, engines of war to throw fire and stones, machines to shoot arrows, and catapults.
[52] The Jews also made engines of war to match theirs, and fought for many days.
[53] But they had no food in storage, because it was the seventh year; those who found safety in Judea from the Gentiles had consumed the last of the stores.
[54] Few men were left in the sanctuary, because famine had prevailed over the rest and they had been scattered, each to his own place.

[55] Then Lysias heard that Philip, whom King Antiochus while still living had appointed to bring up Antiochus his son to be king,
[56] had returned from Persia and Media with the forces that had gone with the king, and that he was trying to seize control of the government.
[57] So he quickly gave orders to depart, and said to the king, to the commanders of the forces, and to the men, "We daily grow weaker, our food supply is scant, the place against which we are fighting is strong, and the affairs of the kingdom press urgently upon us.
[58] Now then let us come to terms with these men, and make peace with them and with all their nation,
[59] and agree to let them live by their laws as they did before; for it was on account of their laws which we abolished that they became angry and did all these things."
[60] The speech pleased the king and the commanders, and he sent to the Jews an offer of peace, and they accepted it.
[61] So the king and the commanders gave them their oath. On these conditions the Jews evacuated the stronghold.
[62] But when the king entered Mount Zion and saw what a strong fortress the place was, he broke the oath he had sworn and gave orders to tear down the wall all around.
[63] Then he departed with haste and returned to Antioch. He found Philip in control of the city, but he fought against him, and took the city by force.
1Mac.7
[1] In the one hundred and fifty-first year Demetrius the son of Seleucus set forth from Rome, sailed with a few men to a city by the sea, and there began to reign.
[2] As he was entering the royal palace of his fathers, the army seized Antiochus and Lysias to bring them to him.
[3] But when this act became known to him, he said, "Do not let me see their faces!"
[4] So the army killed them, and Demetrius took his seat upon the throne of his kingdom.
[5] Then there came to him all the lawless and ungodly men of Israel; they were led by Alcimus, who wanted to be high priest.
[6] And they brought to the king this accusation against the people: "Judas and his brothers have destroyed all your friends, and have driven us out of our land.
[7] Now then send a man whom you trust; let him go and see all the ruin which Judas has brought upon us and upon the land of the king, and let him punish them and all who help them."
[8] So the king chose Bacchides, one of the king's friends, governor of the province Beyond the River; he was a great man in the kingdom and was faithful to the king.

[9] And he sent him, and with him the ungodly Alcimus, whom he made high priest; and he commanded him to take vengeance on the sons of Israel.

[10] So they marched away and came with a large force into the land of Judah; and he sent messengers to Judas and his brothers with peaceable but treacherous words.

[11] But they paid no attention to their words, for they saw that they had come with a large force.

[12] Then a group of scribes appeared in a body before Alcimus and Bacchides to ask for just terms.

[13] The Hasideans were first among the sons of Israel to seek peace from them,

[14] for they said, "A priest of the line of Aaron has come with the army, and he will not harm us."

[15] And he spoke peaceable words to them and swore this oath to them, "We will not seek to injure you or your friends."

[16] So they trusted him; but he seized sixty of them and killed them in one day, in accordance with the word which was written,

[17] "The flesh of thy saints and their blood they poured out round about Jerusalem, and there was none to bury them."

[18] Then the fear and dread of them fell upon all the people, for they said, "There is no truth or justice in them, for they have violated the agreement and the oath which they swore."

[19] Then Bacchides departed from Jerusalem and encamped in Beth-zaith. And he sent and seized many of the men who had deserted to him, and some of the people, and killed them and threw them into a great pit.

[20] He placed Alcimus in charge of the country and left with him a force to help him; then Bacchides went back to the king.

[21] Alcimus strove for the high priesthood,

[22] and all who were troubling their people joined him. They gained control of the land of Judah and did great damage in Israel.

[23] And Judas saw all the evil that Alcimus and those with him had done among the sons of Israel; it was more than the Gentiles had done.

[24] So Judas went out into all the surrounding parts of Judea, and took vengeance on the men who had deserted, and he prevented those in the city from going out into the country.

[25] When Alcimus saw that Judas and those with him had grown strong, and realized that he could not withstand them, he returned to the king and brought wicked charges against them.

[26] Then the king sent Nicanor, one of his honored princes, who hated and detested Israel, and he commanded him to destroy the people.

[27] So Nicanor came to Jerusalem with a large force, and treacherously sent to Judas and his brothers this peaceable message,

[28] "Let there be no fighting between me and you; I shall come with a few men to see you face to face in peace."

[29] So he came to Judas, and they greeted one another peaceably. But the enemy were ready to seize Judas.

[30] It became known to Judas that Nicanor had come to him with treacherous intent, and he was afraid of him and would not meet him again.

[31] When Nicanor learned that his plan had been disclosed, he went out to meet Judas in battle near Caphar-salama.

[32] About five hundred men of the army of Nicanor fell, and the rest fled into the city of David.

[33] After these events Nicanor went up to Mount Zion. Some of the priests came out of the sanctuary, and some of the elders of the people, to greet him peaceably and to show him the burnt offering that was being offered for the king.

[34] But he mocked them and derided them and defiled them and spoke arrogantly,

[35] and in anger he swore this oath, "Unless Judas and his army are delivered into my hands this time, then if I return safely I will burn up this house." And he went out in great anger.

[36] Then the priests went in and stood before the altar and the temple, and they wept and said,

[37] "Thou didst choose this house to be called by thy name, and to be for thy people a house of prayer and supplication.

[38] Take vengeance on this man and on his army, and let them fall by the sword; remember their blasphemies, and let them live no longer."

[39] Now Nicanor went out from Jerusalem and encamped in Beth-horon, and the Syrian army joined him.

[40] And Judas encamped in Adasa with three thousand men. Then Judas prayed and said,

[41] "When the messengers from the king spoke blasphemy, thy angel went forth and struck down one hundred and eighty-five thousand of the Assyrians.

[42] So also crush this army before us today; let the rest learn that Nicanor has spoken wickedly against the sanctuary, and judge him according to this wickedness."

[43] So the armies met in battle on the thirteenth day of the month of Adar. The army of Nicanor was crushed, and he himself was the first to fall in the battle.

[44] When his army saw that Nicanor had fallen, they threw down their arms and fled.

[45] The Jews pursued them a day's journey, from Adasa as far as Gazara, and as they followed kept sounding the battle call on the trumpets.

[46] And men came out of all the villages of Judea round about, and they out-flanked the enemy and drove them back to their pursuers, so that they all fell by the sword; not even one of them was left.
[47] Then the Jews seized the spoils and the plunder, and they cut off Nicanor's head and the right hand which he so arrogantly stretched out, and brought them and displayed them just outside Jerusalem.
[48] The people rejoiced greatly and celebrated that day as a day of great gladness.
[49] And they decreed that this day should be celebrated each year on the thirteenth day of Adar.
[50] So the land of Judah had rest for a few days.
1Mac.8
[1] Now Judas heard of the fame of the Romans, that they were very strong and were well-disposed toward all who made an alliance with them, that they pledged friendship to those who came to them,
[2] and that they were very strong. Men told him of their wars and of the brave deeds which they were doing among the Gauls, how they had defeated them and forced them to pay tribute,
[3] and what they had done in the land of Spain to get control of the silver and gold mines there,
[4] and how they had gained control of the whole region by their planning and patience, even though the place was far distant from them. They also subdued the kings who came against them from the ends of the earth, until they crushed them and inflicted great disaster upon them; the rest paid them tribute every year.
[5] Philip, and Perseus king of the Macedonians, and the others who rose up against them, they crushed in battle and conquered.
[6] They also defeated Antiochus the Great, king of Asia, who went to fight against them with a hundred and twenty elephants and with cavalry and chariots and a very large army. He was crushed by them;
[7] they took him alive and decreed that he and those who should reign after him should pay a heavy tribute and give hostages and surrender some of their best provinces,
[8] the country of India and Media and Lydia. These they took from him and gave to Eumenes the king.
[9] The Greeks planned to come and destroy them,
[10] but this became known to them, and they sent a general against the Greeks and attacked them. Many of them were wounded and fell, and the Romans took captive their wives and children; they plundered them, conquered the land, tore down their strongholds, and enslaved them to this day.
[11] The remaining kingdoms and islands, as many as ever opposed them, they destroyed and enslaved;

[12] but with their friends and those who rely on them they have kept friendship. They have subdued kings far and near, and as many as have heard of their fame have feared them.

[13] Those whom they wish to help and to make kings, they make kings, and those whom they wish they depose; and they have been greatly exalted.

[14] Yet for all this not one of them has put on a crown or worn purple as a mark of pride,

[15] but they have built for themselves a senate chamber, and every day three hundred and twenty senators constantly deliberate concerning the people, to govern them well.

[16] They trust one man each year to rule over them and to control all their land; they all heed the one man, and there is no envy or jealousy among them.

[17] So Judas chose Eupolemus the son of John, son of Accos, and Jason the son of Eleazar, and sent them to Rome to establish friendship and alliance,

[18] and to free themselves from the yoke; for they saw that the kingdom of the Greeks was completely enslaving Israel.

[19] They went to Rome, a very long journey; and they entered the senate chamber and spoke as follows:

[20] "Judas, who is also called Maccabeus, and his brothers and the people of the Jews have sent us to you to establish alliance and peace with you, that we may be enrolled as your allies and friends."

[21] The proposal pleased them,

[22] and this is a copy of the letter which they wrote in reply, on bronze tablets, and sent to Jerusalem to remain with them there as a memorial of peace and alliance:

[23] "May all go well with the Romans and with the nation of the Jews at sea and on land for ever, and may sword and enemy be far from them.

[24] If war comes first to Rome or to any of their allies in all their dominion,

[25] the nation of the Jews shall act as their allies wholeheartedly, as the occasion may indicate to them.

[26] And to the enemy who makes war they shall not give or supply grain, arms, money, or ships, as Rome has decided; and they shall keep their obligations without receiving any return.

[27] In the same way, if war comes first to the nation of the Jews, the Romans shall willingly act as their allies, as the occasion may indicate to them.

[28] And to the enemy allies shall be given no grain, arms, money, or ships, as Rome has decided; and they shall keep these obligations and do so without deceit.

[29] Thus on these terms the Romans make a treaty with the Jewish people.

[30] If after these terms are in effect both parties shall determine to add or delete anything, they shall do so at their discretion, and any addition or deletion that they may make shall be valid.

[31] "And concerning the wrongs which King Demetrius is doing to them we have written to him as follows, `Why have you made your yoke heavy upon our friends and allies the Jews?

[32] If now they appeal again for help against you, we will defend their rights and fight you on sea and on land.'"

1Mac.9

[1] When Demetrius heard that Nicanor and his army had fallen in battle, he sent Bacchides and Alcimus into the land of Judah a second time, and with them the right wing of the army.

[2] They went by the road which leads to Gilgal and encamped against Mesaloth in Arbela, and they took it and killed many people.

[3] In the first month of the one hundred and fifty-second year they encamped against Jerusalem;

[4] then they marched off and went to Berea with twenty thousand foot soldiers and two thousand cavalry.

[5] Now Judas was encamped in Elasa, and with him were three thousand picked men.

[6] When they saw the huge number of the enemy forces, they were greatly frightened, and many slipped away from the camp, until no more than eight hundred of them were left.

[7] When Judas saw that his army had slipped away and the battle was imminent, he was crushed in spirit, for he had no time to assemble them.

[8] He became faint, but he said to those who were left, "Let us rise and go up against our enemies. We may be able to fight them."

[9] But they tried to dissuade him, saying, "We are not able. Let us rather save our own lives now, and let us come back with our brethren and fight them; we are too few."

[10] But Judas said, "Far be it from us to do such a thing as to flee from them. If our time has come, let us die bravely for our brethren, and leave no cause to question our honor."

[11] Then the army of Bacchides marched out from the camp and took its stand for the encounter. The cavalry was divided into two companies, and the slingers and the archers went ahead of the army, as did all the chief warriors.

[12] Bacchides was on the right wing. Flanked by the two companies, the phalanx advanced to the sound of the trumpets; and the men with Judas also blew their trumpets.

[13] The earth was shaken by the noise of the armies, and the battle raged from morning till evening.

[14] Judas saw that Bacchides and the strength of his army were on the right; then all the stouthearted men went with him,

[15] and they crushed the right wing, and he pursued them as far as Mount Azotus.

[16] When those on the left wing saw that the right wing was crushed, they turned and followed close behind Judas and his men.

[17] The battle became desperate, and many on both sides were wounded and fell.

[18] Judas also fell, and the rest fled.

[19] Then Jonathan and Simon took Judas their brother and buried him in the tomb of their fathers at Modein,

[20] and wept for him. And all Israel made great lamentation for him; they mourned many days and said,

[21] "How is the mighty fallen, the savior of Israel!"

[22] Now the rest of the acts of Judas, and his wars and the brave deeds that he did, and his greatness, have not been recorded, for they were very many.

[23] After the death of Judas, the lawless emerged in all parts of Israel; all the doers of injustice appeared.

[24] In those days a very great famine occurred, and the country deserted with them to the enemy.

[25] And Bacchides chose the ungodly and put them in charge of the country.

[26] They sought and searched for the friends of Judas, and brought them to Bacchides, and he took vengeance on them and made sport of them.

[27] Thus there was great distress in Israel, such as had not been since the time that prophets ceased to appear among them.

[28] Then all the friends of Judas assembled and said to Jonathan,

[29] "Since the death of your brother Judas there has been no one like him to go against our enemies and Bacchides, and to deal with those of our nation who hate us.

[30] So now we have chosen you today to take his place as our ruler and leader, to fight our battle."

[31] And Jonathan at that time accepted the leadership and took the place of Judas his brother.

[32] When Bacchides learned of this, he tried to kill him.

[33] But Jonathan and Simon his brother and all who were with him heard of it, and they fled into the wilderness of Tekoa and camped by the water of the pool of Asphar.

[34] Bacchides found this out on the sabbath day, and he with all his army crossed the Jordan.

[35] And Jonathan sent his brother as leader of the multitude and begged the Nabateans, who were his friends, for permission to store with them the great amount of baggage which they had.

[36] But the sons of Jambri from Medeba came out and seized John and all that he had, and departed with it.

[37] After these things it was reported to Jonathan and Simon his brother, "The sons of Jambri are celebrating a great wedding, and are conducting the bride, a daughter of one of the great nobles of Canaan, from Nadabath with a large escort."

[38] And they remembered the blood of John their brother, and went up and hid under cover of the mountain.

[39] They raised their eyes and looked, and saw a tumultuous procession with much baggage; and the bridegroom came out with his friends and his brothers to meet them with tambourines and musicians and many weapons.

[40] Then they rushed upon them from the ambush and began killing them. Many were wounded and fell, and the rest fled to the mountain; and they took all their goods.

[41] Thus the wedding was turned into mourning and the voice of their musicians into a funeral dirge.

[42] And when they had fully avenged the blood of their brother, they returned to the marshes of the Jordan.

[43] When Bacchides heard of this, he came with a large force on the sabbath day to the banks of the Jordan.

[44] And Jonathan said to those with him, "Let us rise up now and fight for our lives, for today things are not as they were before.

[45] For look! the battle is in front of us and behind us; the water of the Jordan is on this side and on that, with marsh and thicket; there is no place to turn.

[46] Cry out now to Heaven that you may be delivered from the hands of our enemies."

[47] So the battle began, and Jonathan stretched out his hand to strike Bacchides, but he eluded him and went to the rear.

[48] Then Jonathan and the men with him leaped into the Jordan and swam across to the other side, and the enemy did not cross the Jordan to attack them.

[49] And about one thousand of Bacchides' men fell that day.

[50] Bacchides then returned to Jerusalem and built strong cities in Judea: the fortress in Jericho, and Emmaus, and Beth-horon, and Bethel, and Timnath, and Pharathon, and Tephon, with high walls and gates and bars.

[51] And he placed garrisons in them to harass Israel.

[52] He also fortified the city of Beth-zur, and Gazara, and the citadel, and in them he put troops and stores of food.

[53] And he took the sons of the leading men of the land as hostages and put them under guard in the citadel at Jerusalem.

[54] In the one hundred and fifty-third year, in the second month, Alcimus gave orders to tear down the wall of the inner court of the sanctuary. He tore down the work of the prophets!

[55] But he only began to tear it down, for at that time Alcimus was stricken and his work was hindered; his mouth was stopped and he was paralyzed, so that he could no longer say a word or give commands concerning his house.

[56] And Alcimus died at that time in great agony.

[57] When Bacchides saw that Alcimus was dead, he returned to the king, and the land of Judah had rest for two years.

[58] Then all the lawless plotted and said, "See! Jonathan and his men are living in quiet and confidence. So now let us bring Bacchides back, and he will capture them all in one night."

[59] And they went and consulted with him.

[60] He started to come with a large force, and secretly sent letters to all his allies in Judea, telling them to seize Jonathan and his men; but they were unable to do it, because their plan became known.

[61] And Jonathan's men seized about fifty of the men of the country who were leaders in this treachery, and killed them.

[62] Then Jonathan with his men, and Simon, withdrew to Bethbasi in the wilderness; he rebuilt the parts of it that had been demolished, and they fortified it.

[63] When Bacchides learned of this, he assembled all his forces, and sent orders to the men of Judea.

[64] Then he came and encamped against Bethbasi; he fought against it for many days and made machines of war.

[65] But Jonathan left Simon his brother in the city, while he went out into the country; and he went with only a few men.

[66] He struck down Odomera and his brothers and the sons of Phasiron in their tents.

[67] Then he began to attack and went into battle with his forces; and Simon and his men sallied out from the city and set fire to the machines of war.

[68] They fought with Bacchides, and he was crushed by them. They distressed him greatly, for his plan and his expedition had been in vain.

[69] So he was greatly enraged at the lawless men who had counseled him to come into the country, and he killed many of them. Then he decided to depart to his own land.

[70] When Jonathan learned of this, he sent ambassadors to him to make peace with him and obtain release of the captives.

[71] He agreed, and did as he said; and he swore to Jonathan that he would not try to harm him as long as he lived.

[72] He restored to him the captives whom he had formerly taken from the land of Judah; then he turned and departed to his own land, and came no more into their territory.

[73] Thus the sword ceased from Israel. And Jonathan dwelt in Michmash. And Jonathan began to judge the people, and he destroyed the ungodly out of Israel.

1Mac.10

[1] In the one hundred and sixtieth year Alexander Epiphanes, the son of Antiochus, landed and occupied Ptolemais. They welcomed him, and there he began to reign.

[2] When Demetrius the king heard of it, he assembled a very large army and marched out to meet him in battle.

[3] And Demetrius sent Jonathan a letter in peaceable words to honor him;

[4] for he said, "Let us act first to make peace with him before he makes peace with Alexander against us,

[5] for he will remember all the wrongs which we did to him and to his brothers and his nation."

[6] So Demetrius gave him authority to recruit troops, to equip them with arms, and to become his ally; and he commanded that the hostages in the citadel should be released to him.

[7] Then Jonathan came to Jerusalem and read the letter in the hearing of all the people and of the men in the citadel.

[8] They were greatly alarmed when they heard that the king had given him authority to recruit troops.

[9] But the men in the citadel released the hostages to Jonathan, and he returned them to their parents.

[10] And Jonathan dwelt in Jerusalem and began to rebuild and restore the city.

[11] He directed those who were doing the work to build the walls and encircle Mount Zion with squared stones, for better fortification; and they did so.

[12] Then the foreigners who were in the strongholds that Bacchides had built fled;

[13] each left his place and departed to his own land.

[14] Only in Beth-zur did some remain who had forsaken the law and the commandments, for it served as a place of refuge.

[15] Now Alexander the king heard of all the promises which Demetrius had sent to Jonathan, and men told him of the battles that Jonathan and his brothers had fought, of the brave deeds that they had done, and of the troubles that they had endured.

[16] So he said, "Shall we find another such man? Come now, we will make him our friend and ally."

[17] And he wrote a letter and sent it to him, in the following words:

[18] "King Alexander to his brother Jonathan, greeting.

[19] We have heard about you, that you are a mighty warrior and worthy to be our friend.

[20] And so we have appointed you today to be the high priest of your nation; you are to be called the king's friend" (and he sent him a purple robe and a golden crown) "and you are to take our side and keep friendship with us."

[21] So Jonathan put on the holy garments in the seventh month of the one hundred and sixtieth year, at the feast of tabernacles, and he recruited troops and equipped them with arms in abundance.

[22] When Demetrius heard of these things he was grieved and said,

[23] "What is this that we have done? Alexander has gotten ahead of us in forming a friendship with the Jews to strengthen himself.

[24] I also will write them words of encouragement and promise them honor and gifts, that I may have their help."

[25] So he sent a message to them in the following words: "King Demetrius to the nation of the Jews, greeting.

[26] Since you have kept your agreement with us and have continued your friendship with us, and have not sided with our enemies, we have heard of it and rejoiced.

[27] And now continue still to keep faith with us, and we will repay you with good for what you do for us.

[28] We will grant you many immunities and give you gifts.

[29] "And now I free you and exempt all the Jews from payment of tribute and salt tax and crown levies,

[30] and instead of collecting the third of the grain and the half of the fruit of the trees that I should receive, I release them from this day and henceforth. I will not collect them from the land of Judah or from the three districts added to it from Samaria and Galilee, from this day and for all time.

[31] And let Jerusalem and her environs, her tithes and her revenues, be holy and free from tax.

[32] I release also my control of the citadel in Jerusalem and give it to the high priest, that he may station in it men of his own choice to guard it.

[33] And every one of the Jews taken as a captive from the land of Judah into any part of my kingdom, I set free without payment; and let all officials cancel also the taxes on their cattle.

[34] "And all the feasts and sabbaths and new moons and appointed days, and the three days before a feast and the three after a feast -- let them all be days of immunity and release for all the Jews who are in my kingdom.

[35] No one shall have authority to exact anything from them or annoy any of them about any matter.

[36] "Let Jews be enrolled in the king's forces to the number of thirty thousand men, and let the maintenance be given them that is due to all the forces of the king.

[37] Let some of them be stationed in the great strongholds of the king, and let some of them be put in positions of trust in the kingdom. Let their

officers and leaders be of their own number, and let them live by their own laws, just as the king has commanded in the land of Judah.

[38] "As for the three districts that have been added to Judea from the country of Samaria, let them be so annexed to Judea that they are considered to be under one ruler and obey no other authority but the high priest.

[39] Ptolemais and the land adjoining it I have given as a gift to the sanctuary in Jerusalem, to meet the necessary expenses of the sanctuary.

[40] I also grant fifteen thousand shekels of silver yearly out of the king's revenues from appropriate places.

[41] And all the additional funds which the government officials have not paid as they did in the first years, they shall give from now on for the service of the temple.

[42] Moreover, the five thousand shekels of silver which my officials have received every year from the income of the services of the temple, this too is canceled, because it belongs to the priests who minister there.

[43] And whoever takes refuge at the temple in Jerusalem, or in any of its precincts, because he owes money to the king or has any debt, let him be released and receive back all his property in my kingdom.

[44] "Let the cost of rebuilding and restoring the structures of the sanctuary be paid from the revenues of the king.

[45] And let the cost of rebuilding the walls of Jerusalem and fortifying it round about, and the cost of rebuilding the walls in Judea, also be paid from the revenues of the king."

[46] When Jonathan and the people heard these words, they did not believe or accept them, because they remembered the great wrongs which Demetrius had done in Israel and how he had greatly oppressed them.

[47] They favored Alexander, because he had been the first to speak peaceable words to them, and they remained his allies all his days.

[48] Now Alexander the king assembled large forces and encamped opposite Demetrius.

[49] The two kings met in battle, and the army of Demetrius fled, and Alexander pursued him and defeated them.

[50] He pressed the battle strongly until the sun set, and Demetrius fell on that day.

[51] Then Alexander sent ambassadors to Ptolemy king of Egypt with the following message:

[52] "Since I have returned to my kingdom and have taken my seat on the throne of my fathers, and established my rule -- for I crushed Demetrius and gained control of our country;

[53] I met him in battle, and he and his army were crushed by us, and we have taken our seat on the throne of his kingdom --

[54] now therefore let us establish friendship with one another; give me now your daughter as my wife, and I will become your son-in-law, and will make gifts to you and to her in keeping with your position."

[55] Ptolemy the king replied and said, "Happy was the day on which you returned to the land of your fathers and took your seat on the throne of their kingdom.

[56] And now I will do for you as you wrote, but meet me at Ptolemais, so that we may see one another, and I will become your father-in-law, as you have said."

[57] So Ptolemy set out from Egypt, he and Cleopatra his daughter, and came to Ptolemais in the one hundred and sixty-second year.

[58] Alexander the king met him, and Ptolemy gave him Cleopatra his daughter in marriage, and celebrated her wedding at Ptolemais with great pomp, as kings do.

[59] Then Alexander the king wrote to Jonathan to come to meet him.

[60] So he went with pomp to Ptolemais and met the two kings; he gave them and their friends silver and gold and many gifts, and found favor with them.

[61] A group of pestilent men from Israel, lawless men, gathered together against him to accuse him; but the king paid no attention to them.

[62] The king gave orders to take off Jonathan's garments and to clothe him in purple, and they did so.

[63] The king also seated him at his side; and he said to his officers, "Go forth with him into the middle of the city and proclaim that no one is to bring charges against him about any matter, and let no one annoy him for any reason."

[64] And when his accusers saw the honor that was paid him, in accordance with the proclamation, and saw him clothed in purple, they all fled.

[65] Thus the king honored him and enrolled him among his chief friends, and made him general and governor of the province.

[66] And Jonathan returned to Jerusalem in peace and gladness.

[67] In the one hundred and sixty-fifth year Demetrius the son of Demetrius came from Crete to the land of his fathers.

[68] When Alexander the king heard of it, he was greatly grieved and returned to Antioch.

[69] And Demetrius appointed Apollonius the governor of Coelesyria, and he assembled a large force and encamped against Jamnia. Then he sent the following message to Jonathan the high priest:

[70] "You are the only one to rise up against us, and I have become a laughingstock and reproach because of you. Why do you assume authority against us in the hill country?

[71] If you now have confidence in your forces, come down to the plain to meet us, and let us match strength with each other there, for I have with me the power of the cities.

[72] Ask and learn who I am and who the others are that are helping us. Men will tell you that you cannot stand before us, for your fathers were twice put to flight in their own land.

[73] And now you will not be able to withstand my cavalry and such an army in the plain, where there is no stone or pebble, or place to flee."

[74] When Jonathan heard the words of Apollonius, his spirit was aroused. He chose ten thousand men and set out from Jerusalem, and Simon his brother met him to help him.

[75] He encamped before Joppa, but the men of the city closed its gates, for Apollonius had a garrison in Joppa.

[76] So they fought against it, and the men of the city became afraid and opened the gates, and Jonathan gained possession of Joppa.

[77] When Apollonius heard of it, he mustered three thousand cavalry and a large army, and went to Azotus as though he were going farther. At the same time he advanced into the plain, for he had a large troop of cavalry and put confidence in it.

[78] Jonathan pursued him to Azotus, and the armies engaged in battle.

[79] Now Apollonius had secretly left a thousand cavalry behind them.

[80] Jonathan learned that there was an ambush behind him, for they surrounded his army and shot arrows at his men from early morning till late afternoon.

[81] But his men stood fast, as Jonathan commanded, and the enemy's horses grew tired.

[82] Then Simon brought forward his force and engaged the phalanx in battle (for the cavalry was exhausted); they were overwhelmed by him and fled,

[83] and the cavalry was dispersed in the plain. They fled to Azotus and entered Beth-dagon, the temple of their idol, for safety.

[84] But Jonathan burned Azotus and the surrounding towns and plundered them; and the temple of Dagon, and those who had taken refuge in it he burned with fire.

[85] The number of those who fell by the sword, with those burned alive, came to eight thousand men.

[86] Then Jonathan departed from there and encamped against Askalon, and the men of the city came out to meet him with great pomp.

[87] And Jonathan and those with him returned to Jerusalem with much booty.

[88] When Alexander the king heard of these things, he honored Jonathan still more;

[89] and he sent to him a golden buckle, such as it is the custom to give to the kinsmen of kings. He also gave him Ekron and all its environs as his possession.

1Mac.11

[1] Then the king of Egypt gathered great forces, like the sand by the seashore, and many ships; and he tried to get possession of Alexander's kingdom by trickery and add it to his own kingdom.

[2] He set out for Syria with peaceable words, and the people of the cities opened their gates to him and went to meet him, for Alexander the king had commanded them to meet him, since he was Alexander's father-in-law.

[3] But when Ptolemy entered the cities he stationed forces as a garrison in each city.

[4] When he approached Azotus, they showed him the temple of Dagon burned down, and Azotus and its suburbs destroyed, and the corpses lying about, and the charred bodies of those whom Jonathan had burned in the war, for they had piled them in heaps along his route.

[5] They also told the king what Jonathan had done, to throw blame on him; but the king kept silent.

[6] Jonathan met the king at Joppa with pomp, and they greeted one another and spent the night there.

[7] And Jonathan went with the king as far as the river called Eleutherus; then he returned to Jerusalem.

[8] So King Ptolemy gained control of the coastal cities as far as Seleucia by the sea, and he kept devising evil designs against Alexander.

[9] He sent envoys to Demetrius the king, saying, "Come, let us make a covenant with each other, and I will give you in marriage my daughter who was Alexander's wife, and you shall reign over your father's kingdom.

[10] For I now regret that I gave him my daughter, for he has tried to kill me."

[11] He threw blame on Alexander because he coveted his kingdom.

[12] So he took his daughter away from him and gave her to Demetrius. He was estranged from Alexander, and their enmity became manifest.

[13] Then Ptolemy entered Antioch and put on the crown of Asia. Thus he put two crowns upon his head, the crown of Egypt and that of Asia.

[14] Now Alexander the king was in Cilicia at that time, because the people of that region were in revolt.

[15] And Alexander heard of it and came against him in battle. Ptolemy marched out and met him with a strong force, and put him to flight.

[16] So Alexander fled into Arabia to find protection there, and King Ptolemy was exalted.

[17] And Zabdiel the Arab cut off the head of Alexander and sent it to Ptolemy.

[18] But King Ptolemy died three days later, and his troops in the strongholds were killed by the inhabitants of the strongholds.
[19] So Demetrius became king in the one hundred and sixty-seventh year.
[20] In those days Jonathan assembled the men of Judea to attack the citadel in Jerusalem, and he built many engines of war to use against it.
[21] But certain lawless men who hated their nation went to the king and reported to him that Jonathan was besieging the citadel.
[22] When he heard this he was angry, and as soon as he heard it he set out and came to Ptolemais; and he wrote Jonathan not to continue the siege, but to meet him for a conference at Ptolemais as quickly as possible.
[23] When Jonathan heard this, he gave orders to continue the siege; and he chose some of the elders of Israel and some of the priests, and put himself in danger,
[24] for he went to the king at Ptolemais, taking silver and gold and clothing and numerous other gifts. And he won his favor.
[25] Although certain lawless men of his nation kept making complaints against him,
[26] the king treated him as his predecessors had treated him; he exalted him in the presence of all his friends.
[27] He confirmed him in the high priesthood and in as many other honors as he had formerly had, and made him to be regarded as one of his chief friends.
[28] Then Jonathan asked the king to free Judea and the three districts of Samaria from tribute, and promised him three hundred talents.
[29] The king consented, and wrote a letter to Jonathan about all these things; its contents were as follows:
[30] "King Demetrius to Jonathan his brother and to the nation of the Jews, greeting.
[31] This copy of the letter which we wrote concerning you to Lasthenes our kinsman we have written to you also, so that you may know what it says.
[32] `King Demetrius to Lasthenes his father, greeting.
[33] To the nation of the Jews, who are our friends and fulfil their obligations to us, we have determined to do good, because of the good will they show toward us.
[34] We have confirmed as their possession both the territory of Judea and the three districts of Aphairema and Lydda and Rathamin; the latter, with all the region bordering them, were added to Judea from Samaria. To all those who offer sacrifice in Jerusalem, we have granted release from the royal taxes which the king formerly received from them each year, from the crops of the land and the fruit of the trees.
[35] And the other payments henceforth due to us of the tithes, and the taxes due to us, and the salt pits and the crown taxes due to us -- from all these we shall grant them release.

[36] And not one of these grants shall be canceled from this time forth for ever.

[37] Now therefore take care to make a copy of this, and let it be given to Jonathan and put up in a conspicuous place on the holy mountain.'"

[38] Now when Demetrius the king saw that the land was quiet before him and that there was no opposition to him, he dismissed all his troops, each man to his own place, except the foreign troops which he had recruited from the islands of the nations. So all the troops who had served his fathers hated him.

[39] Now Trypho had formerly been one of Alexander's supporters. He saw that all the troops were murmuring against Demetrius. So he went to Imalkue the Arab, who was bringing up Antiochus, the young son of Alexander,

[40] and insistently urged him to hand Antiochus over to him, to become king in place of his father. He also reported to Imalkue what Demetrius had done and told of the hatred which the troops of Demetrius had for him; and he stayed there many days.

[41] Now Jonathan sent to Demetrius the king the request that he remove the troops of the citadel from Jerusalem, and the troops in the strongholds; for they kept fighting against Israel.

[42] And Demetrius sent this message to Jonathan, "Not only will I do these things for you and your nation, but I will confer great honor on you and your nation, if I find an opportunity.

[43] Now then you will do well to send me men who will help me, for all my troops have revolted."

[44] So Jonathan sent three thousand stalwart men to him at Antioch, and when they came to the king, the king rejoiced at their arrival.

[45] Then the men of the city assembled within the city, to the number of a hundred and twenty thousand, and they wanted to kill the king.

[46] But the king fled into the palace. Then the men of the city seized the main streets of the city and began to fight.

[47] So the king called the Jews to his aid, and they all rallied about him and then spread out through the city; and they killed on that day as many as a hundred thousand men.

[48] They set fire to the city and seized much spoil on that day, and they saved the king.

[49] When the men of the city saw that the Jews had gained control of the city as they pleased, their courage failed and they cried out to the king with this entreaty,

[50] "Grant us peace, and make the Jews stop fighting against us and our city."

[51] And they threw down their arms and made peace. So the Jews gained glory in the eyes of the king and of all the people in his kingdom, and they returned to Jerusalem with much spoil.

[52] So Demetrius the king sat on the throne of his kingdom, and the land was quiet before him.

[53] But he broke his word about all that he had promised; and he became estranged from Jonathan and did not repay the favors which Jonathan had done him, but oppressed him greatly.

[54] After this Trypho returned, and with him the young boy Antiochus who began to reign and put on the crown.

[55] All the troops that Demetrius had cast off gathered around him, and they fought against Demetrius, and he fled and was routed.

[56] And Trypho captured the elephants and gained control of Antioch.

[57] Then the young Antiochus wrote to Jonathan, saying, "I confirm you in the high priesthood and set you over the four districts and make you one of the friends of the king."

[58] And he sent him gold plate and a table service, and granted him the right to drink from gold cups and dress in purple and wear a gold buckle.

[59] Simon his brother he made governor from the Ladder of Tyre to the borders of Egypt.

[60] Then Jonathan set forth and traveled beyond the river and among the cities, and all the army of Syria gathered to him as allies. When he came to Askalon, the people of the city met him and paid him honor.

[61] From there he departed to Gaza, but the men of Gaza shut him out. So he beseiged it and burned its suburbs with fire and plundered them.

[62] Then the people of Gaza pleaded with Jonathan, and he made peace with them, and took the sons of their rulers as hostages and sent them to Jerusalem. And he passed through the country as far as Damascus.

[63] Then Jonathan heard that the officers of Demetrius had come to Kadesh in Galilee with a large army, intending to remove him from office.

[64] He went to meet them, but left his brother Simon in the country.

[65] Simon encamped before Beth-zur and fought against it for many days and hemmed it in.

[66] Then they asked him to grant them terms of peace, and he did so. He removed them from there, took possession of the city, and set a garrison over it.

[67] Jonathan and his army encamped by the waters of Gennesaret. Early in the morning they marched to the plain of Hazor,

[68] and behold, the army of the foreigners met him in the plain; they had set an ambush against him in the mountains, but they themselves met him face to face.

[69] Then the men in ambush emerged from their places and joined battle.

[70] All the men with Jonathan fled; not one of them was left except Mattathias the son of Absalom and Judas the son of Chalphi, commanders of the forces of the army.

[71] Jonathan rent his garments and put dust on his head, and prayed.

[72] Then he turned back to the battle against the enemy and routed them, and they fled.

[73] When his men who were fleeing saw this, they returned to him and joined him in the pursuit as far as Kadesh, to their camp, and there they encamped.

[74] As many as three thousand of the foreigners fell that day. And Jonathan returned to Jerusalem.

1Mac.12

[1] Now when Jonathan saw that the time was favorable for him, he chose men and sent them to Rome to confirm and renew the friendship with them.

[2] He also sent letters to the same effect to the Spartans and to other places.

[3] So they went to Rome and entered the senate chamber and said, "Jonathan the high priest and the Jewish nation have sent us to renew the former friendship and alliance with them."

[4] And the Romans gave them letters to the people in every place, asking them to provide for the envoys safe conduct to the land of Judah.

[5] This is a copy of the letter which Jonathan wrote to the Spartans:

[6] "Jonathan the high priest, the senate of the nation, the priests, and the rest of the Jewish people to their brethren the Spartans, greeting.

[7] Already in time past a letter was sent to Onias the high priest from Arius, who was king among you, stating that you are our brethren, as the appended copy shows.

[8] Onias welcomed the envoy with honor, and received the letter, which contained a clear declaration of alliance and friendship.

[9] Therefore, though we have no need of these things, since we have as encouragement the holy books which are in our hands,

[10] we have undertaken to send to renew our brotherhood and friendship with you, so that we may not become estranged from you, for considerable time has passed since you sent your letter to us.

[11] We therefore remember you constantly on every occasion, both in our feasts and on other appropriate days, at the sacrifices which we offer and in our prayers, as it is right and proper to remember brethren.

[12] And we rejoice in your glory.

[13] But as for ourselves, many afflictions and many wars have encircled us; the kings round about us have waged war against us.

[14] We were unwilling to annoy you and our other allies and friends with these wars,

[15] for we have the help which comes from Heaven for our aid; and we were delivered from our enemies and our enemies were humbled.

[16] We therefore have chosen Numenius the son of Antiochus and Antipater the son of Jason, and have sent them to Rome to renew our former friendship and alli ance with them.

[17] We have commanded them to go also to you and greet you and deliver to you this letter from us concerning the renewal of our brotherhood.
[18] And now please send us a reply to this."
[19] This is a copy of the letter which they sent to Onias:
[20] "Arius, king of the Spartans, to Onias the high priest, greeting.
[21] It has been found in writing concerning the Spartans and the Jews that they are brethren and are of the family of Abraham.
[22] And now that we have learned this, please write us concerning your welfare;
[23] we on our part write to you that your cattle and your property belong to us, and ours belong to you. We therefore command that our envoys report to you accordingly."
[24] Now Jonathan heard that the commanders of Demetrius had returned, with a larger force than before, to wage war against him.
[25] So he marched away from Jerusalem and met them in the region of Hamath, for he gave them no opportunity to invade his own country.
[26] He sent spies to their camp, and they returned and reported to him that the enemy were being drawn up in formation to fall upon the Jews by night.
[27] So when the sun set, Jonathan commanded his men to be alert and to keep their arms at hand so as to be ready all night for battle, and he stationed outposts around the camp.
[28] When the enemy heard that Jonathan and his men were prepared for battle, they were afraid and were terrified at heart; so they kindled fires in their camp and withdrew.
[29] But Jonathan and his men did not know it until morning, for they saw the fires burning.
[30] Then Jonathan pursued them, but he did not overtake them, for they had crossed the Eleutherus river.
[31] So Jonathan turned aside against the Arabs who are called Zabadeans, and he crushed them and plundered them.
[32] Then he broke camp and went to Damascus, and marched through all that region.
[33] Simon also went forth and marched through the country as far as Askalon and the neighboring strongholds. He turned aside to Joppa and took it by surprise,
[34] for he had heard that they were ready to hand over the stronghold to the men whom Demetrius had sent. And he stationed a garrison there to guard it.
[35] When Jonathan returned he convened the elders of the people and planned with them to build strongholds in Judea,

[36] to build the walls of Jerusalem still higher, and to erect a high barrier between the citadel and the city to separate it from the city, in order to isolate it so that its garrison could neither buy nor sell.

[37] So they gathered together to build up the city; part of the wall on the valley to the east had fallen, and he repaired the section called Chaphenatha.

[38] And Simon built Adida in the Shephelah; he fortified it and installed gates with bolts.

[39] Then Trypho attempted to become king in Asia and put on the crown, and to raise his hand against Antiochus the king.

[40] He feared that Jonathan might not permit him to do so, but might make war on him, so he kept seeking to seize and kill him, and he marched forth and came to Beth-shan.

[41] Jonathan went out to meet him with forty thousand picked fighting men, and he came to Beth-shan.

[42] When Trypho saw that he had come with a large army, he was afraid to raise his hand against him.

[43] So he received him with honor and commended him to all his friends, and he gave him gifts and commanded his friends and his troops to obey him as they would himself.

[44] Then he said to Jonathan, "Why have you wearied all these people when we are not at war?

[45] Dismiss them now to their homes and choose for yourself a few men to stay with you, and come with me to Ptolemais. I will hand it over to you as well as the other strongholds and the remaining troops and all the officials, and will turn round and go home. For that is why I am here."

[46] Jonathan trusted him and did as he said; he sent away the troops, and they returned to the land of Judah.

[47] He kept with himself three thousand men, two thousand of whom he left in Galilee, while a thousand accompanied him.

[48] But when Jonathan entered Ptolemais, the men of Ptolemais closed the gates and seized him, and all who had entered with him they killed with the sword.

[49] Then Trypho sent troops and cavalry into Galilee and the Great Plain to destroy all Jonathan's soldiers.

[50] But they realized that Jonathan had been seized and had perished along with his men, and they encouraged one another and kept marching in close formation, ready for battle.

[51] When their pursuers saw that they would fight for their lives, they turned back.

[52] So they all reached the land of Judah safely, and they mourned for Jonathan and his companions and were in great fear; and all Israel mourned deeply.

[53] And all the nations round about them tried to destroy them, for they said, "They have no leader or helper. Now therefore let us make war on them and blot out the memory of them from among men."
1Mac.13
[1] Simon heard that Trypho had assembled a large army to invade the land of Judah and destroy it,
[2] and he saw that the people were trembling and fearful. So he went up to Jerusalem, and gathering the people together
[3] he encouraged them, saying to them, "You yourselves know what great things I and my brothers and the house of my father have done for the laws and the sanctuary; you know also the wars and the difficulties which we have seen.
[4] By reason of this all my brothers have perished for the sake of Israel, and I alone am left.
[5] And now, far be it from me to spare my life in any time of distress, for I am not better than my brothers.
[6] But I will avenge my nation and the sanctuary and your wives and children, for all the nations have gathered together out of hatred to destroy us."
[7] The spirit of the people was rekindled when they heard these words,
[8] and they answered in a loud voice, "You are our leader in place of Judas and Jonathan your brother.
[9] Fight our battles, and all that you say to us we will do."
[10] So he assembled all the warriors and hastened to complete the walls of Jerusalem, and he fortified it on every side.
[11] He sent Jonathan the son of Absalom to Joppa, and with him a considerable army; he drove out its occupants and remained there.
[12] Then Trypho departed from Ptolemais with a large army to invade the land of Judah, and Jonathan was with him under guard.
[13] And Simon encamped in Adida, facing the plain.
[14] Trypho learned that Simon had risen up in place of Jonathan his brother, and that he was about to join battle with him, so he sent envoys to him and said,
[15] "It is for the money that Jonathan your brother owed the royal treasury, in connection with the offices he held, that we are detaining him.
[16] Send now a hundred talents of silver and two of his sons as hostages, so that when released he will not revolt against us, and we will release him."
[17] Simon knew that they were speaking deceitfully to him, but he sent to get the money and the sons, lest he arouse great hostility among the people, who might say,
[18] "Because Simon did not send him the money and the sons, he perished."

[19] So he sent the sons and the hundred talents, but Trypho broke his word and did not release Jonathan.

[20] After this Trypho came to invade the country and destroy it, and he circled around by the way to Adora. But Simon and his army kept marching along opposite him to every place he went.

[21] Now the men in the citadel kept sending envoys to Trypho urging him to come to them by way of the wilderness and to send them food.

[22] So Trypho got all his cavalry ready to go, but that night a very heavy snow fell, and he did not go because of the snow. He marched off and went into the land of Gilead.

[23] When he approached Baskama, he killed Jonathan, and he was buried there.

[24] Then Trypho turned back and departed to his own land.

[25] And Simon sent and took the bones of Jonathan his brother, and buried him in Modein, the city of his fathers.

[26] All Israel bewailed him with great lamentation, and mourned for him many days.

[27] And Simon built a monument over the tomb of his father and his brothers; he made it high that it might be seen, with polished stone at the front and back.

[28] He also erected seven pyramids, opposite one another, for his father and mother and four brothers.

[29] And for the pyramids he devised an elaborate setting, erecting about them great columns, and upon the columns he put suits of armor for a permanent memorial, and beside the suits of armor carved ships, so that they could be seen by all who sail the sea.

[30] This is the tomb which he built in Modein; it remains to this day.

[31] Trypho dealt treacherously with the young king Antiochus; he killed him

[32] and became king in his place, putting on the crown of Asia; and he brought great calamity upon the land.

[33] But Simon built up the strongholds of Judea and walled them all around, with high towers and great walls and gates and bolts, and he stored food in the strongholds.

[34] Simon also chose men and sent them to Demetrius the king with a request to grant relief to the country, for all that Trypho did was to plunder.

[35] Demetrius the king sent him a favorable reply to this request, and wrote him a letter as follows,

[36] "King Demetrius to Simon, the high priest and friend of kings, and to the elders and nation of the Jews, greeting.

[37] We have received the gold crown and the palm branch which you sent, and we are ready to make a general peace with you and to write to our officials to grant you release from tribute.

[38] All the grants that we have made to you remain valid, and let the strongholds that you have built be your possession.

[39] We pardon any errors and offenses committed to this day, and cancel the crown tax which you owe; and whatever other tax has been collected in Jerusalem shall be collected no longer.

[40] And if any of you are qualified to be enrolled in our bodyguard, let them be enrolled, and let there be peace between us."

[41] In the one hundred and seventieth year the yoke of the Gentiles was removed from Israel,

[42] and the people began to write in their documents and contracts, "In the first year of Simon the great high priest and commander and leader of the Jews."

[43] In those days Simon encamped against Gazara and surrounded it with troops. He made a siege engine, brought it up to the city, and battered and captured one tower.

[44] The men in the siege engine leaped out into the city, and a great tumult arose in the city.

[45] The men in the city, with their wives and children, went up on the wall with their clothes rent, and they cried out with a loud voice, asking Simon to make peace with them;

[46] they said, "Do not treat us according to our wicked acts but according to your mercy."

[47] So Simon reached an agreement with them and stopped fighting against them. But he expelled them from the city and cleansed the houses in which the idols were, and then entered it with hymns and praise.

[48] He cast out of it all uncleanness, and settled in it men who observed the law. He also strengthened its fortifications and built in it a house for himself.

[49] The men in the citadel at Jerusalem were prevented from going out to the country and back to buy and sell. So they were very hungry, and many of them perished from famine.

[50] Then they cried to Simon to make peace with them, and he did so. But he expelled them from there and cleansed the citadel from its pollutions.

[51] On the twenty-third day of the second month, in the one hundred and seventy-first year, the Jews entered it with praise and palm branches, and with harps and cymbals and stringed instruments, and with hymns and songs, because a great enemy had been crushed and removed from Israel.

[52] And Simon decreed that every year they should celebrate this day with rejoicing. He strengthened the fortifications of the temple hill alongside the citadel, and he and his men dwelt there.

[53] And Simon saw that John his son had reached manhood, so he made him commander of all the forces, and he dwelt in Gazara.

1Mac.14

[1] In the one hundred and seventy-second year Demetrius the king assembled his forces and marched into Media to secure help, so that he could make war against Trypho.

[2] When Arsaces the king of Persia and Media heard that Demetrius had invaded his territory, he sent one of his commanders to take him alive.

[3] And he went and defeated the army of Demetrius, and seized him and took him to Arsaces, who put him under guard.

[4] The land had rest all the days of Simon. He sought the good of his nation; his rule was pleasing to them, as was the honor shown him, all his days.

[5] To crown all his honors he took Joppa for a harbor, and opened a way to the isles of the sea.

[6] He extended the borders of his nation, and gained full control of the country.

[7] He gathered a host of captives; he ruled over Gazara and Beth-zur and the citadel, and he removed its uncleanness from it; and there was none to oppose him.

[8] They tilled their land in peace; the ground gave its increase, and the trees of the plains their fruit.

[9] Old men sat in the streets; they all talked together of good things; and the youths donned the glories and garments of war.

[10] He supplied the cities with food, and furnished them with the means of defense, till his renown spread to the ends of the earth.

[11] He established peace in the land, and Israel rejoiced with great joy.

[12] Each man sat under his vine and his fig tree, and there was none to make them afraid.

[13] No one was left in the land to fight them, and the kings were crushed in those days.

[14] He strengthened all the humble of his people; he sought out the law, and did away with every lawless and wicked man.

[15] He made the sanctuary glorious, and added to the vessels of the sanctuary.

[16] It was heard in Rome, and as far away as Sparta, that Jonathan had died, and they were deeply grieved.

[17] When they heard that Simon his brother had become high priest in his place, and that he was ruling over the country and the cities in it,

[18] they wrote to him on bronze tablets to renew with him the friendship and alliance which they had established with Judas and Jonathan his brothers.

[19] And these were read before the assembly in Jerusalem.

[20] This is a copy of the letter which the Spartans sent: "The rulers and the city of the Spartans to Simon the high priest and to the elders and the priests and the rest of the Jewish people, our brethren, greeting.

[21] The envoys who were sent to our people have told us about your glory and honor, and we rejoiced at their coming.

[22] And what they said we have recorded in our public decrees, as follows, `Numenius the son of Antiochus and Antipater the son of Jason, envoys of the Jews, have come to us to renew their friendship with us.

[23] It has pleased our people to receive these men with honor and to put a copy of their words in the public archives, so that the people of the Spartans may have a record of them. And they have sent a copy of this to Simon the high priest.'"

[24] After this Simon sent Numenius to Rome with a large gold shield weighing a thousand minas, to confirm the alliance with the Romans.

[25] When the people heard these things they said, "How shall we thank Simon and his sons?

[26] For he and his brothers and the house of his father have stood firm; they have fought and repulsed Israel's enemies and established its freedom."

[27] So they made a record on bronze tablets and put it upon pillars on Mount Zion. This is a copy of what they wrote: "On the eighteenth day of Elul, in the one hundred and seventy-second year, which is the third year of Simon the great high priest,

[28] in Asaramel, in the great assembly of the priests and the people and the rulers of the nation and the elders of the country, the following was proclaimed to us:

[29] "Since wars often occurred in the country, Simon the son of Mattathias, a priest of the sons of Joarib, and his brothers, exposed themselves to danger and resisted the enemies of their nation, in order that their sanctuary and the law might be perserved; and they brought great glory to their nation.

[30] Jonathan rallied the nation, and became their high priest, and was gathered to his people.

[31] And when their enemies decided to invade their country and lay hands on their sanctuary,

[32] then Simon rose up and fought for his nation. He spent great sums of his own money; he armed the men of his nation's forces and paid them wages.

[33] He fortified the cities of Judea, and Beth-zur on the borders of Judea, where formerly the arms of the enemy had been stored, and he placed there a garrison of Jews.

[34] He also fortified Joppa, which is by the sea, and Gazara, which is on the borders of Azotus, where the enemy formerly dwelt. He settled Jews there, and provided in those cities whatever was necessary for their restoration.

[35] "The people saw Simon's faithfulness and the glory which he had resolved to win for his nation, and they made him their leader and high

priest, because he had done all these things and because of the justice and loyalty which he had maintained toward his nation. He sought in every way to exalt his people.

[36] And in his days things prospered in his hands, so that the Gentiles were put out of the country, as were also the men in the city of David in Jerusalem, who had built themselves a citadel from which they used to sally forth and defile the environs of the sanctuary and do great damage to its purity.

[37] He settled Jews in it, and fortified it for the safety of the country and of the city, and built the walls of Jerusalem higher.

[38] "In view of these things King Demetrius confirmed him in the high priesthood,

[39] and he made him one of the king's friends and paid him high honors.

[40] For he had heard that the Jews were addressed by the Romans as friends and allies and brethren, and that the Romans had received the envoys of Simon with honor.

[41] "And the Jews and their priests decided that Simon should be their leader and high priest for ever, until a trustworthy prophet should arise,

[42] and that he should be governor over them and that he should take charge of the sanctuary and appoint men over its tasks and over the country and the weapons and the strongholds, and that he should take charge of the sanctuary,

[43] and that he should be obeyed by all, and that all contracts in the country should be written in his name, and that he should be clothed in purple and wear gold.

[44] "And none of the people or priests shall be permitted to nullify any of these decisions or to oppose what he says, or to convene an assembly in the country without his permission, or to be clothed in purple or put on a gold buckle.

[45] Whoever acts contrary to these decisions or nullifies any of them shall be liable to punishment."

[46] And all the people agreed to grant Simon the right to act in accord with these decisions.

[47] So Simon accepted and agreed to be high priest, to be commander and ethnarch of the Jews and priests, and to be protector of them all.

[48] And they gave orders to inscribe this decree upon bronze tablets, to put them up in a conspicuous place in the precincts of the sanctuary,

[49] and to deposit copies of them in the treasury, so that Simon and his sons might have them.

1Mac.15

[1] Antiochus, the son of Demetrius the king, sent a letter from the islands of the sea to Simon, the priest and ethnarch of the Jews, and to all the nation;

[2] its contents were as follows: "King Antiochus to Simon the high priest and ethnarch and to the nation of the Jews, greeting.
[3] Whereas certain pestilent men have gained control of the kingdom of our fathers, and I intend to lay claim to the kingdom so that I may restore it as it formerly was, and have recruited a host of mercenary troops and have equipped warships,
[4] and intend to make a landing in the country so that I may proceed against those who have destroyed our country and those who have devastated many cities in my kingdom,
[5] now therefore I confirm to you all the tax remissions that the kings before me have granted you, and release from all the other payments from which they have released you.
[6] I permit you to mint your own coinage as money for your country,
[7] and I grant freedom to Jerusalem and the sanctuary. All the weapons which you have prepared and the strongholds which you have built and now hold shall remain yours.
[8] Every debt you owe to the royal treasury and any such future debts shall be canceled for you from henceforth and for all time.
[9] When we gain control of our kingdom, we will bestow great honor upon you and your nation and the temple, so that your glory will become manifest in all the earth."
[10] In the one hundred and seventy-fourth year Antiochus set out and invaded the land of his fathers. All the troops rallied to him, so that there were few with Trypho.
[11] Antiochus pursued him, and he came in his flight to Dor, which is by the sea;
[12] for he knew that troubles had converged upon him, and his troops had deserted him.
[13] So Antiochus encamped against Dor, and with him were a hundred and twenty thousand warriors and eight thousand cavalry.
[14] He surrounded the city, and the ships joined battle from the sea; he pressed the city hard from land and sea, and permitted no one to leave or enter it.
[15] Then Numenius and his companions arrived from Rome, with letters to the kings and countries, in which the following was written:
[16] "Lucius, consul of the Romans, to King Ptolemy, greeting.
[17] The envoys of the Jews have come to us as our friends and allies to renew our ancient friendship and alliance. They had been sent by Simon the high priest and by the people of the Jews,
[18] and have brought a gold shield weighing a thousand minas.
[19] We therefore have decided to write to the kings and countries that they should not seek their harm or make war against them and their cities and their country, or make alliance with those who war against them.
[20] And it has seemed good to us to accept the shield from them.

[21] Therefore if any pestilent men have fled to you from their country, hand them over to Simon the high priest, that he may punish them according to their law."

[22] The consul wrote the same thing to Demetrius the king and to Attalus and Ariarathes and Arsaces,

[23] and to all the countries, and to Sampsames, and to the Spartans, and to Delos, and to Myndos, and to Sicyon, and to Caria, and to Samos, and to Pamphylia, and to Lycia, and to Halicarnassus, and to Rhodes, and to Phaselis, and to Cos, and to Side, and to Aradus and Gortyna and Cnidus and Cyprus and Cyrene.

[24] They also sent a copy of these things to Simon the high priest.

[25] Antiochus the king besieged Dor anew, continually throwing his forces against it and making engines of war; and he shut Trypho up and kept him from going out or in.

[26] And Simon sent to Antiochus two thousand picked men, to fight for him, and silver and gold and much military equipment.

[27] But he refused to receive them, and he broke all the agreements he formerly had made with Simon, and became estranged from him.

[28] He sent to him Athenobius, one of his friends, to confer with him, saying, "You hold control of Joppa and Gazara and the citadel in Jerusalem; they are cities of my kingdom.

[29] You have devastated their territory, you have done great damage in the land, and you have taken possession of many places in my kingdom.

[30] Now then, hand over the cities which you have seized and the tribute money of the places which you have conquered outside the borders of Judea;

[31] or else give me for them five hundred talents of silver, and for the destruction that you have caused and the tribute money of the cities, five hundred talents more. Otherwise we will come and conquer you."

[32] So Athenobius the friend of the king came to Jerusalem, and when he saw the splendor of Simon, and the sideboard with its gold and silver plate, and his great magnificence, he was amazed. He reported to him the words of the king,

[33] but Simon gave him this reply: "We have neither taken foreign land nor seized foreign property, but only the inheritance of our fathers, which at one time had been unjustly taken by our enemies.

[34] Now that we have the opportunity, we are firmly holding the inheritance of our fathers.

[35] As for Joppa and Gazara, which you demand, they were causing great damage among the people and to our land; for them we will give you a hundred talents." Athenobius did not answer him a word,

[36] but returned in wrath to the king and reported to him these words and the splendor of Simon and all that he had seen. And the king was greatly angered.

[37] Now Trypho embarked on a ship and escaped to Orthosia.

[38] Then the king made Cendebeus commander-in-chief of the coastal country, and gave him troops of infantry and cavalry.

[39] He commanded him to encamp against Judea, and commanded him to build up Kedron and fortify its gates, and to make war on the people; but the king pursued Trypho.

[40] So Cendebeus came to Jamnia and began to provoke the people and invade Judea and take the people captive and kill them.

[41] He built up Kedron and stationed there horsemen and troops, so that they might go out and make raids along the highways of Judea, as the king had ordered him.

1Mac.16

[1] John went up from Gazara and reported to Simon his father what Cendebeus had done.

[2] And Simon called in his two older sons Judas and John, and said to them: "I and my brothers and the house of my father have fought the wars of Israel from our youth until this day, and things have prospered in our hands so that we have delivered Israel many times.

[3] But now I have grown old, and you by His mercy are mature in years. Take my place and my brother's, and go out and fight for our nation, and may the help which comes from Heaven be with you."

[4] So John chose out of the country twenty thousand warriors and horsemen, and they marched against Cendebeus and camped for the night in Modein.

[5] Early in the morning they arose and marched into the plain, and behold, a large force of infantry and horsemen was coming to meet them; and a stream lay between them.

[6] Then he and his army lined up against them. And he saw that the soldiers were afraid to cross the stream, so he crossed over first; and when his men saw him, they crossed over after him.

[7] Then he divided the army and placed the horsemen in the midst of the infantry, for the cavalry of the enemy were very numerous.

[8] And they sounded the trumpets, and Cendebeus and his army were put to flight, and many of them were wounded and fell; the rest fled into the stronghold.

[9] At that time Judas the brother of John was wounded, but John pursued them until Cendebeus reached Kedron, which he had built.

[10] They also fled into the towers that were in the fields of Azotus, and John burned it with fire, and about two thousand of them fell. And he returned to Judea safely.

[11] Now Ptolemy the son of Abubus had been appointed governor over the plain of Jericho, and he had much silver and gold,

[12] for he was son-in-law of the high priest.

[13] His heart was lifted up; he determined to get control of the country, and made treacherous plans against Simon and his sons, to do away with them.

[14] Now Simon was visiting the cities of the country and attending to their needs, and he went down to Jericho with Mattathias and Judas his sons, in the one hundred and seventy-seventh year, in the eleventh month, which is the month of Shebat.

[15] The son of Abubus received them treacherously in the little stronghold called Dok, which he had built; he gave them a great banquet, and hid men there.

[16] When Simon and his sons were drunk, Ptolemy and his men rose up, took their weapons, and rushed in against Simon in the banquet hall, and they killed him and his two sons and some of his servants.

[17] So he committed an act of great treachery and returned evil for good.

[18] Then Ptolemy wrote a report about these things and sent it to the king, asking him to send troops to aid him and to turn over to him the cities and the country.

[19] He sent other men to Gazara to do away with John; he sent letters to the captains asking them to come to him so that he might give them silver and gold and gifts;

[20] and he sent other men to take possession of Jerusalem and the temple hill.

[21] But some one ran ahead and reported to John at Gazara that his father and brothers had perished, and that "he has sent men to kill you also."

[22] When he heard this, he was greatly shocked; and he seized the men who came to destroy him and killed them, for he had found out that they were seeking to destroy him.

[23] The rest of the acts of John and his wars and the brave deeds which he did, and the building of the walls which he built, and his achievements,

[24] behold, they are written in the chronicles of his high priesthood, from the time that he became high priest after his father.

2 Maccabees

2Mac.1

[1] The Jewish brethren in Jerusalem and those in the land of Judea, To their Jewish brethren in Egypt, Greeting, and good peace.

[2] May God do good to you, and may he remember his covenant with Abraham and Isaac and Jacob, his faithful servants.

[3] May he give you all a heart to worship him and to do his will with a strong heart and a willing spirit.

[4] May he open your heart to his law and his commandments, and may he bring peace.

[5] May he hear your prayers and be reconciled to you, and may he not forsake you in time of evil.

[6] We are now praying for you here.

[7] In the reign of Demetrius, in the one hundred and sixty-ninth year, we Jews wrote to you, in the critical distress which came upon us in those years after Jason and his company revolted from the holy land and the kingdom

[8] and burned the gate and shed innocent blood. We besought the Lord and we were heard, and we offered sacrifice and cereal offering, and we lighted the lamps and we set out the loaves.

[9] And now see that you keep the feast of booths in the month of Chislev, in the one hundred and eighty-eighth year.

[10] Those in Jerusalem and those in Judea and the senate and Judas, To Aristobulus, who is of the family of the anointed priests, teacher of Ptolemy the king, and to the Jews in Egypt, Greeting, and good health.

[11] Having been saved by God out of grave dangers we thank him greatly for taking our side against the king.

[12] For he drove out those who fought against the holy city.

[13] For when the leader reached Persia with a force that seemed irresistible, they were cut to pieces in the temple of Nanea by a deception employed by the priests of Nanea.

[14] For under pretext of intending to marry her, Antiochus came to the place together with his friends, to secure most of its treasures as a dowry.

[15] When the priests of the temple of Nanea had set out the treasures and Antiochus had come with a few men inside the wall of the sacred precinct, they closed the temple as soon as he entered it.

[16] Opening the secret door in the ceiling, they threw stones and struck down the leader and his men, and dismembered them and cut off their heads and threw them to the people outside.

[17] Blessed in every way be our God, who has brought judgment upon those who have behaved impiously.

[18] Since on the twenty-fifth day of Chislev we shall celebrate the purification of the temple, we thought it necessary to notify you, in order that you also may celebrate the feast of booths and the feast of the fire given when Nehemiah, who built the temple and the altar, offered sacrifices.

[19] For when our fathers were being led captive to Persia, the pious priests of that time took some of the fire of the altar and secretly hid it in the hollow of a dry cistern, where they took such precautions that the place was unknown to any one.

[20] But after many years had passed, when it pleased God, Nehemiah, having been commissioned by the king of Persia, sent the descendants of the priests who had hidden the fire to get it. And when they reported to us that they had not found fire but thick liquid, he ordered them to dip it out and bring it.

[21] And when the materials for the sacrifices were presented, Nehemiah ordered the priests to sprinkle the liquid on the wood and what was laid upon it.

[22] When this was done and some time had passed and the sun, which had been clouded over, shone out, a great fire blazed up, so that all marveled.

[23] And while the sacrifice was being consumed, the priests offered prayer -- the priests and every one. Jonathan led, and the rest responded, as did Nehemiah.

[24] The prayer was to this effect:

"O Lord, Lord God, Creator of all things, who art awe-inspiring and strong and just and merciful, who alone art King and art kind, [25] who alone art bountiful, who alone art just and almighty and eternal, who do rescue Israel from every evil, who didst choose the fathers and consecrate them, [26] accept this sacrifice on behalf of all thy people Israel and preserve thy portion and make it holy. [27] Gather together our scattered people, set free those who are slaves among the Gentiles, look upon those who are rejected and despised, and let the Gentiles know that thou art our God. [28] Afflict those who oppress and are insolent with pride. [29] Plant thy people in thy holy place, as Moses said." [30] Then the priests sang the hymns. [31] And when the materials of the sacrifice were consumed, Nehemiah ordered that the liquid that was left should be poured upon large stones. [32] When this was done, a flame blazed up; but when the light from the altar shone back, it went out. [33] When this matter became known, and it was reported to the king of the Persians that, in the place where the exiled priests had hidden the fire, the liquid had appeared with which Nehemiah and his associates had burned the materials of the sacrifice, [34] the king investigated the matter, and enclosed the place and made it sacred. [35] And with those persons whom the king favored he exchanged many excellent gifts. [36] Nehemiah and his associates called this "nephthar," which means purification, but by most people it is called naphtha.

2Mac.2

[1] One finds in the records that Jeremiah the prophet ordered those who were being deported to take some of the fire, as has been told,

[2] and that the prophet after giving them the law instructed those who were being deported not to forget the commandments of the Lord, nor to be led astray in their thoughts upon seeing the gold and silver statues and their adornment.

[3] And with other similar words he exhorted them that the law should not depart from their hearts.

[4] It was also in the writing that the prophet, having received an oracle, ordered that the tent and the ark should follow with him, and that he went out to the mountain where Moses had gone up and had seen the inheritance of God.

[5] And Jeremiah came and found a cave, and he brought there the tent and the ark and the altar of incense, and he sealed up the entrance.

[6] Some of those who followed him came up to mark the way, but could not find it.

[7] When Jeremiah learned of it, he rebuked them and declared: "The place shall be unknown until God gathers his people together again and shows his mercy.

[8] And then the Lord will disclose these things, and the glory of the Lord and the cloud will appear, as they were shown in the case of Moses, and as Solomon asked that the place should be specially consecrated."

[9] It was also made clear that being possessed of wisdom Solomon offered sacrifice for the dedication and completion of the temple.

[10] Just as Moses prayed to the Lord, and fire came down from heaven and devoured the sacrifices, so also Solomon prayed, and the fire came down and consumed the whole burnt offerings.

[11] And Moses said, "They were consumed because the sin offering had not been eaten."

[12] Likewise Solomon also kept the eight days.

[13] The same things are reported in the records and in the memoirs of Nehemiah, and also that he founded a library and collected the books about the kings and prophets, and the writings of David, and letters of kings about votive offerings.

[14] In the same way Judas also collected all the books that had been lost on account of the war which had come upon us, and they are in our possession.

[15] So if you have need of them, send people to get them for you.

[16] Since, therefore, we are about to celebrate the purification, we write to you. Will you therefore please keep the days?

[17] It is God who has saved all his people, and has returned the inheritance to all, and the kingship and priesthood and consecration,
[18] as he promised through the law. For we have hope in God that he will soon have mercy upon us and will gather us from everywhere under heaven into his holy place, for he has rescued us from great evils and has purified the place.
[19] The story of Judas Maccabeus and his brothers, and the purification of the great temple, and the dedication of the altar,
[20] and further the wars against Antiochus Epiphanes and his son Eupator,
[21] and the appearances which came from heaven to those who strove zealously on behalf of Judaism, so that though few in number they seized the whole land and pursued the barbarian hordes,
[22] and recovered the temple famous throughout the world and freed the city and restored the laws that were about to be abolished, while the Lord with great kindness became gracious to them --
[23] all this, which has been set forth by Jason of Cyrene in five volumes, we shall attempt to condense into a single book.
[24] For considering the flood of numbers involved and the difficulty there is for those who wish to enter upon the narratives of history because of the mass of material,
[25] we have aimed to please those who wish to read, to make it easy for those who are inclined to memorize, and to profit all readers.
[26] For us who have undertaken the toil of abbreviating, it is no light matter but calls for sweat and loss of sleep,
[27] just as it is not easy for one who prepares a banquet and seeks the benefit of others. However, to secure the gratitude of many we will gladly endure the uncomfortable toil,
[28] leaving the responsibility for exact details to the compiler, while devoting our effort to arriving at the outlines of the condensation.
[29] For as the master builder of a new house must be concerned with the whole construction, while the one who undertakes its painting and decoration has to consider only what is suitable for its adornment, such in my judgment is the case with us.
[30] It is the duty of the original historian to occupy the ground and to discuss matters from every side and to take trouble with details,
[31] but the one who recasts the narrative should be allowed to strive for brevity of expression and to forego exhaustive treatment.
[32] At this point therefore let us begin our narrative, adding only so much to what has already been said; for it is foolish to lengthen the preface while cutting short the history itself.
2Mac.3

[1] While the holy city was inhabited in unbroken peace and the laws were very well observed because of the piety of the high priest Onias and his hatred of wickedness,

[2] it came about that the kings themselves honored the place and glorified the temple with the finest presents,

[3] so that even Seleucus, the king of Asia, defrayed from his own revenues all the expenses connected with the service of the sacrifices.

[4] But a man named Simon, of the tribe of Benjamin, who had been made captain of the temple, had a disagreement with the high priest about the administration of the city market;

[5] and when he could not prevail over Onias he went to Apollonius of Tarsus, who at that time was governor of Coelesyria and Phoenicia.

[6] He reported to him that the treasury in Jerusalem was full of untold sums of money, so that the amount of the funds could not be reckoned, and that they did not belong to the account of the sacrifices, but that it was possible for them to fall under the control of the king.

[7] When Apollonius met the king, he told him of the money about which he had been informed. The king chose Heliodorus, who was in charge of his affairs, and sent him with commands to effect the removal of the aforesaid money.

[8] Heliodorus at once set out on his journey, ostensibly to make a tour of inspection of the cities of Coelesyria and Phoenicia, but in fact to carry out the king's purpose.

[9] When he had arrived at Jerusalem and had been kindly welcomed by the high priest of the city, he told about the disclosure that had been made and stated why he had come, and he inquired whether this really was the situation.

[10] The high priest explained that there were some deposits belonging to widows and orphans,

[11] and also some money of Hyrcanus, son of Tobias, a man of very prominent position, and that it totaled in all four hundred talents of silver and two hundred of gold. To such an extent the impious Simon had misrepresented the facts.

[12] And he said that it was utterly impossible that wrong should be done to those people who had trusted in the holiness of the place and in the sanctity and inviolability of the temple which is honored throughout the whole world.

[13] But Heliodorus, because of the king's commands which he had, said that this money must in any case be confiscated for the king's treasury.

[14] So he set a day and went in to direct the inspection of these funds. There was no little distress throughout the whole city.

[15] The priests prostrated themselves before the altar in their priestly garments and called toward heaven upon him who had given the law

about deposits, that he should keep them safe for those who had deposited them.

[16] To see the appearance of the high priest was to be wounded at heart, for his face and the change in his color disclosed the anguish of his soul.

[17] For terror and bodily trembling had come over the man, which plainly showed to those who looked at him the pain lodged in his heart.

[18] People also hurried out of their houses in crowds to make a general supplication because the holy place was about to be brought into contempt.

[19] Women, girded with sackcloth under their breasts, thronged the streets. Some of the maidens who were kept indoors ran together to the gates, and some to the walls, while others peered out of the windows.

[20] And holding up their hands to heaven, they all made entreaty.

[21] There was something pitiable in the prostration of the whole populace and the anxiety of the high priest in his great anguish.

[22] While they were calling upon the Almighty Lord that he would keep what had been entrusted safe and secure for those who had entrusted it,

[23] Heliodorus went on with what had been decided.

[24] But when he arrived at the treasury with his bodyguard, then and there the Sovereign of spirits and of all authority caused so great a manifestation that all who had been so bold as to accompany him were astounded by the power of God, and became faint with terror.

[25] For there appeared to them a magnificently caparisoned horse, with a rider of frightening mien, and it rushed furiously at Heliodorus and struck at him with its front hoofs. Its rider was seen to have armor and weapons of gold.

[26] Two young men also appeared to him, remarkably strong, gloriously beautiful and splendidly dressed, who stood on each side of him and scourged him continuously, inflicting many blows on him.

[27] When he suddenly fell to the ground and deep darkness came over him, his men took him up and put him on a stretcher

[28] and carried him away, this man who had just entered the aforesaid treasury with a great retinue and all his bodyguard but was now unable to help himself; and they recognized clearly the sovereign power of God.

[29] While he lay prostrate, speechless because of the divine intervention and deprived of any hope of recovery,

[30] they praised the Lord who had acted marvelously for his own place. And the temple, which a little while before was full of fear and disturbance, was filled with joy and gladness, now that the Almighty Lord had appeared.

[31] Quickly some of Heliodorus' friends asked Onias to call upon the Most High and to grant life to one who was lying quite at his last breath.

[32] And the high priest, fearing that the king might get the notion that some foul play had been perpetrated by the Jews with regard to Heliodorus, offered sacrifice for the man's recovery.

[33] While the high priest was making the offering of atonement, the same young men appeared again to Heliodorus dressed in the same clothing, and they stood and said, "Be very grateful to Onias the high priest, since for his sake the Lord has granted you your life.

[34] And see that you, who have been scourged by heaven, report to all men the majestic power of God." Having said this they vanished.

[35] Then Heliodorus offered sacrifice to the Lord and made very great vows to the Savior of his life, and having bidden Onias farewell, he marched off with his forces to the king.

[36] And he bore testimony to all men of the deeds of the supreme God, which he had seen with his own eyes.

[37] When the king asked Heliodorus what sort of person would be suitable to send on another mission to Jerusalem, he replied,

[38] "If you have any enemy or plotter against your government, send him there, for you will get him back thoroughly scourged, if he escapes at all, for there certainly is about the place some power of God.

[39] For he who has his dwelling in heaven watches over that place himself and brings it aid, and he strikes and destroys those who come to do it injury."

[40] This was the outcome of the episode of Heliodorus and the protection of the treasury.

2Mac.4

[1] The previously mentioned Simon, who had informed about the money against his own country, slandered Onias, saying that it was he who had incited Heliodorus and had been the real cause of the misfortune.

[2] He dared to designate as a plotter against the government the man who was the benefactor of the city, the protector of his fellow countrymen, and a zealot for the laws.

[3] When his hatred progressed to such a degree that even murders were committed by one of Simon's approved agents,

[4] Onias recognized that the rivalry was serious and that Apollonius, the son of Menestheus and governor of Coelesyria and Phoenicia, was intensifying the malice of Simon.

[5] So he betook himself to the king, not accusing his fellow citizens but having in view the welfare, both public and private, of all the people.

[6] For he saw that without the king's attention public affairs could not again reach a peaceful settlement, and that Simon would not stop his folly.

[7] When Seleucus died and Antiochus who was called Epiphanes succeeded to the kingdom, Jason the brother of Onias obtained the high priesthood by corruption,

[8] promising the king at an interview three hundred and sixty talents of silver and, from another source of revenue, eighty talents.

[9] In addition to this he promised to pay one hundred and fifty more if permission were given to establish by his authority a gymnasium and a body of youth for it, and to enrol the men of Jerusalem as citizens of Antioch.

[10] When the king assented and Jason came to office, he at once shifted his countrymen over to the Greek way of life.

[11] He set aside the existing royal concessions to the Jews, secured through John the father of Eupolemus, who went on the mission to establish friendship and alliance with the Romans; and he destroyed the lawful ways of living and introduced new customs contrary to the law.

[12] For with alacrity he founded a gymnasium right under the citadel, and he induced the noblest of the young men to wear the Greek hat.

[13] There was such an extreme of Hellenization and increase in the adoption of foreign ways because of the surpassing wickedness of Jason, who was ungodly and no high priest,

[14] that the priests were no longer intent upon their service at the altar. Despising the sanctuary and neglecting the sacrifices, they hastened to take part in the unlawful proceedings in the wrestling arena after the call to the discus,

[15] disdaining the honors prized by their fathers and putting the highest value upon Greek forms of prestige.

[16] For this reason heavy disaster overtook them, and those whose ways of living they admired and wished to imitate completely became their enemies and punished them.

[17] For it is no light thing to show irreverence to the divine laws -- a fact which later events will make clear.

[18] When the quadrennial games were being held at Tyre and the king was present,

[19] the vile Jason sent envoys, chosen as being Antiochian citizens from Jerusalem, to carry three hundred silver drachmas for the sacrifice to Hercules. Those who carried the money, however, thought best not to use it for sacrifice, because that was inappropriate, but to expend it for another purpose.

[20] So this money was intended by the sender for the sacrifice to Hercules, but by the decision of its carriers it was applied to the construction of triremes.

[21] When Apollonius the son of Menestheus was sent to Egypt for the coronation of Philometor as king, Antiochus learned that Philometor had become hostile to his government, and he took measures for his own security. Therefore upon arriving at Joppa he proceeded to Jerusalem.

[22] He was welcomed magnificently by Jason and the city, and ushered in with a blaze of torches and with shouts. Then he marched into Phoenicia.

[23] After a period of three years Jason sent Menelaus, the brother of the previously mentioned Simon, to carry the money to the king and to complete the records of essential business.
[24] But he, when presented to the king, extolled him with an air of authority, and secured the high priesthood for himself, outbidding Jason by three hundred talents of silver.
[25] After receiving the king's orders he returned, possessing no qualification for the high priesthood, but having the hot temper of a cruel tyrant and the rage of a savage wild beast.
[26] So Jason, who after supplanting his own brother was supplanted by another man, was driven as a fugitive into the land of Ammon.
[27] And Menelaus held the office, but he did not pay regularly any of the money promised to the king.
[28] When Sostratus the captain of the citadel kept requesting payment, for the collection of the revenue was his responsibility, the two of them were summoned by the king on account of this issue.
[29] Menelaus left his own brother Lysimachus as deputy in the high priesthood, while Sostratus left Crates, the commander of the Cyprian troops.
[30] While such was the state of affairs, it happened that the people of Tarsus and of Mallus revolted because their cities had been given as a present to Antiochis, the king's concubine.
[31] So the king went hastily to settle the trouble, leaving Andronicus, a man of high rank, to act as his deputy.
[32] But Menelaus, thinking he had obtained a suitable opportunity, stole some of the gold vessels of the temple and gave them to Andronicus; other vessels, as it happened, he had sold to Tyre and the neighboring cities.
[33] When Onias became fully aware of these acts he publicly exposed them, having first withdrawn to a place of sanctuary at Daphne near Antioch.
[34] Therefore Menelaus, taking Andronicus aside, urged him to kill Onias. Andronicus came to Onias, and resorting to treachery offered him sworn pledges and gave him his right hand, and in spite of his suspicion persuaded Onias to come out from the place of sanctuary; then, with no regard for justice, he immediately put him out of the way.
[35] For this reason not only Jews, but many also of other nations, were grieved and displeased at the unjust murder of the man.
[36] When the king returned from the region of Cilicia, the Jews in the city appealed to him with regard to the unreasonable murder of Onias, and the Greeks shared their hatred of the crime.
[37] Therefore Antiochus was grieved at heart and filled with pity, and wept because of the moderation and good conduct of the deceased;
[38] and inflamed with anger, he immediately stripped off the purple robe from Andronicus, tore off his garments, and led him about the whole city

to that very place where he had committed the outrage against Onias, and there he dispatched the bloodthirsty fellow. The Lord thus repaid him with the punishment he deserved.

[39] When many acts of sacrilege had been committed in the city by Lysimachus with the connivance of Menelaus, and when report of them had spread abroad, the populace gathered against Lysimachus, because many of the gold vessels had already been stolen.

[40] And since the crowds were becoming aroused and filled with anger, Lysimachus armed about three thousand men and launched an unjust attack, under the leadership of a certain Auranus, a man advanced in years and no less advanced in folly.

[41] But when the Jews became aware of Lysimachus' attack, some picked up stones, some blocks of wood, and others took handfuls of the ashes that were lying about, and threw them in wild confusion at Lysimachus and his men.

[42] As a result, they wounded many of them, and killed some, and put them all to flight; and the temple robber himself they killed close by the treasury.

[43] Charges were brought against Menelaus about this incident.

[44] When the king came to Tyre, three men sent by the senate presented the case before him.

[45] But Menelaus, already as good as beaten, promised a substantial bribe to Ptolemy son of Dorymenes to win over the king.

[46] Therefore Ptolemy, taking the king aside into a colonnade as if for refreshment, induced the king to change his mind.

[47] Menelaus, the cause of all the evil, he acquitted of the charges against him, while he sentenced to death those unfortunate men, who would have been freed uncondemned if they had pleaded even before Scythians.

[48] And so those who had spoken for the city and the villages and the holy vessels quickly suffered the unjust penalty.

[49] Therefore even the Tyrians, showing their hatred of the crime, provided magnificently for their funeral.

[50] But Menelaus, because of the cupidity of those in power, remained in office, growing in wickedness, having become the chief plotter against his fellow citizens.

2Mac.5

[1] About this time Antiochus made his second invasion of Egypt.

[2] And it happened that over all the city, for almost forty days, there appeared golden-clad horsemen charging through the air, in companies fully armed with lances and drawn swords --

[3] troops of horsemen drawn up, attacks and counterattacks made on this side and on that, brandishing of shields, massing of spears, hurling of missiles, the flash of golden trappings, and armor of all sorts.

[4] Therefore all men prayed that the apparition might prove to have been a good omen.

[5] When a false rumor arose that Antiochus was dead, Jason took no less than a thousand men and suddenly made an assault upon the city. When the troops upon the wall had been forced back and at last the city was being taken, Menelaus took refuge in the citadel.

[6] But Jason kept relentlessly slaughtering his fellow citizens, not realizing that success at the cost of one's kindred is the greatest misfortune, but imagining that he was setting up trophies of victory over enemies and not over fellow countrymen.

[7] He did not gain control of the government, however; and in the end got only disgrace from his conspiracy, and fled again into the country of the Ammonites.

[8] Finally he met a miserable end. Accused before Aretas the ruler of the Arabs, fleeing from city to city, pursued by all men, hated as a rebel against the laws, and abhorred as the executioner of his country and his fellow citizens, he was cast ashore in Egypt;

[9] and he who had driven many from their own country into exile died in exile, having embarked to go to the Lacedaemonians in hope of finding protection because of their kinship.

[10] He who had cast out many to lie unburied had no one to mourn for him; he had no funeral of any sort and no place in the tomb of his fathers.

[11] When news of what had happened reached the king, he took it to mean that Judea was in revolt. So, raging inwardly, he left Egypt and took the city by storm.

[12] And he commanded his soldiers to cut down relentlessly every one they met and to slay those who went into the houses.

[13] Then there was killing of young and old, destruction of boys, women, and children, and slaughter of virgins and infants.

[14] Within the total of three days eighty thousand were destroyed, forty thousand in hand-to-hand fighting; and as many were sold into slavery as were slain.

[15] Not content with this, Antiochus dared to enter the most holy temple in all the world, guided by Menelaus, who had become a traitor both to the laws and to his country.

[16] He took the holy vessels with his polluted hands, and swept away with profane hands the votive offerings which other kings had made to enhance the glory and honor of the place.

[17] Antiochus was elated in spirit, and did not perceive that the Lord was angered for a little while because of the sins of those who dwelt in the city, and that therefore he was disregarding the holy place.

[18] But if it had not happened that they were involved in many sins, this man would have been scourged and turned back from his rash act as soon

as he came forward, just as Heliodorus was, whom Seleucus the king sent to inspect the treasury.

[19] But the Lord did not choose the nation for the sake of the holy place, but the place for the sake of the nation.

[20] Therefore the place itself shared in the misfortunes that befell the nation and afterward participated in its benefits; and what was forsaken in the wrath of the Almighty was restored again in all its glory when the great Lord became reconciled.

[21] So Antiochus carried off eighteen hundred talents from the temple, and hurried away to Antioch, thinking in his arrogance that he could sail on the land and walk on the sea, because his mind was elated.

[22] And he left governors to afflict the people: at Jerusalem, Philip, by birth a Phrygian and in character more barbarous than the man who appointed him;

[23] and at Gerizim, Andronicus; and besides these Menelaus, who lorded it over his fellow citizens worse than the others did. In his malice toward the Jewish citizens,

[24] Antiochus sent Apollonius, the captain of the Mysians, with an army of twenty-two thousand, and commanded him to slay all the grown men and to sell the women and boys as slaves.

[25] When this man arrived in Jerusalem, he pretended to be peaceably disposed and waited until the holy sabbath day; then, finding the Jews not at work, he ordered his men to parade under arms.

[26] He put to the sword all those who came out to see them, then rushed into the city with his armed men and killed great numbers of people.

[27] But Judas Maccabeus, with about nine others, got away to the wilderness, and kept himself and his companions alive in the mountains as wild animals do; they continued to live on what grew wild, so that they might not share in the defilement.

2Mac.6

[1] Not long after this, the king sent an Athenian senator to compel the Jews to forsake the laws of their fathers and cease to live by the laws of God,

[2] and also to pollute the temple in Jerusalem and call it the temple of Olympian Zeus, and to call the one in Gerizim the temple of Zeus the Friend of Strangers, as did the people who dwelt in that place.

[3] Harsh and utterly grievous was the onslaught of evil.

[4] For the temple was filled with debauchery and reveling by the Gentiles, who dallied with harlots and had intercourse with women within the sacred precincts, and besides brought in things for sacrifice that were unfit.

[5] The altar was covered with abominable offerings which were forbidden by the laws.

[6] A man could neither keep the sabbath, nor observe the feasts of his fathers, nor so much as confess himself to be a Jew.

[7] On the monthly celebration of the king's birthday, the Jews were taken, under bitter constraint, to partake of the sacrifices; and when the feast of Dionysus came, they were compelled to walk in the procession in honor of Dionysus, wearing wreaths of ivy.

[8] At the suggestion of Ptolemy a decree was issued to the neighboring Greek cities, that they should adopt the same policy toward the Jews and make them partake of the sacrifices,

[9] and should slay those who did not choose to change over to Greek customs. One could see, therefore, the misery that had come upon them.

[10] For example, two women were brought in for having circumcised their children. These women they publicly paraded about the city, with their babies hung at their breasts, then hurled them down headlong from the wall.

[11] Others who had assembled in the caves near by, to observe the seventh day secretly, were betrayed to Philip and were all burned together, because their piety kept them from defending themselves, in view of their regard for that most holy day.

[12] Now I urge those who read this book not to be depressed by such calamities, but to recognize that these punishments were designed not to destroy but to discipline our people.

[13] In fact, not to let the impious alone for long, but to punish them immediately, is a sign of great kindness.

[14] For in the case of the other nations the Lord waits patiently to punish them until they have reached the full measure of their sins; but he does not deal in this way with us,

[15] in order that he may not take vengeance on us afterward when our sins have reached their height.

[16] Therefore he never withdraws his mercy from us. Though he disciplines us with calamities, he does not forsake his own people.

[17] Let what we have said serve as a reminder; we must go on briefly with the story.

[18] Eleazar, one of the scribes in high position, a man now advanced in age and of noble presence, was being forced to open his mouth to eat swine's flesh.

[19] But he, welcoming death with honor rather than life with pollution, went up to the the rack of his own accord, spitting out the flesh,

[20] as men ought to go who have the courage to refuse things that it is not right to taste, even for the natural love of life.

[21] Those who were in charge of that unlawful sacrifice took the man aside, because of their long acquaintance with him, and privately urged him to bring meat of his own providing, proper for him to use, and pretend that he was eating the flesh of the sacrificial meal which had been commanded by the king,

[22] so that by doing this he might be saved from death, and be treated kindly on account of his old friendship with them.

[23] But making a high resolve, worthy of his years and the dignity of his old age and the gray hairs which he had reached with distinction and his excellent life even from childhood, and moreover according to the holy God-given law, he declared himself quickly, telling them to send him to Hades.

[24] "Such pretense is not worthy of our time of life," he said, "lest many of the young should suppose that Eleazar in his ninetieth year has gone over to an alien religion,

[25] and through my pretense, for the sake of living a brief moment longer, they should be led astray because of me, while I defile and disgrace my old age.

[26] For even if for the present I should avoid the punishment of men, yet whether I live or die I shall not escape the hands of the Almighty.

[27] Therefore, by manfully giving up my life now, I will show myself worthy of my old age

[28] and leave to the young a noble example of how to die a good death willingly and nobly for the revered and holy laws." When he had said this, he went at once to the rack.

[29] And those who a little before had acted toward him with good will now changed to ill will, because the words he had uttered were in their opinion sheer madness.

[30] When he was about to die under the blows, he groaned aloud and said: "It is clear to the Lord in his holy knowledge that, though I might have been saved from death, I am enduring terrible sufferings in my body under this beating, but in my soul I am glad to suffer these things because I fear him."

[31] So in this way he died, leaving in his death an example of nobility and a memorial of courage, not only to the young but to the great body of his nation.

2Mac.7

[1] It happened also that seven brothers and their mother were arrested and were being compelled by the king, under torture with whips and cords, to partake of unlawful swine's flesh.

[2] One of them, acting as their spokesman, said, "What do you intend to ask and learn from us? For we are ready to die rather than transgress the laws of our fathers."

[3] The king fell into a rage, and gave orders that pans and caldrons be heated.

[4] These were heated immediately, and he commanded that the tongue of their spokesman be cut out and that they scalp him and cut off his hands and feet, while the rest of the brothers and the mother looked on.

[5] When he was utterly helpless, the king ordered them to take him to the fire, still breathing, and to fry him in a pan. The smoke from the pan spread widely, but the brothers and their mother encouraged one another to die nobly, saying,

[6] "The Lord God is watching over us and in truth has compassion on us, as Moses declared in his song which bore witness against the people to their faces, when he said, `And he will have compassion on his servants.'"

[7] After the first brother had died in this way, they brought forward the second for their sport. They tore off the skin of his head with the hair, and asked him, "Will you eat rather than have your body punished limb by limb?"

[8] He replied in the language of his fathers, and said to them, "No." Therefore he in turn underwent tortures as the first brother had done.

[9] And when he was at his last breath, he said, "You accursed wretch, you dismiss us from this present life, but the King of the universe will raise us up to an everlasting renewal of life, because we have died for his laws."

[10] After him, the third was the victim of their sport. When it was demanded, he quickly put out his tongue and courageously stretched forth his hands,

[11] and said nobly, "I got these from Heaven, and because of his laws I disdain them, and from him I hope to get them back again."

[12] As a result the king himself and those with him were astonished at the young man's spirit, for he regarded his sufferings as nothing.

[13] When he too had died, they maltreated and tortured the fourth in the same way.

[14] And when he was near death, he said, "One cannot but choose to die at the hands of men and to cherish the hope that God gives of being raised again by him. But for you there will be no resurrection to life!"

[15] Next they brought forward the fifth and maltreated him.

[16] But he looked at the king, and said, "Because you have authority among men, mortal though you are, you do what you please. But do not think that God has forsaken our people.

[17] Keep on, and see how his mighty power will torture you and your descendants!"

[18] After him they brought forward the sixth. And when he was about to die, he said, "Do not deceive yourself in vain. For we are suffering these things on our own account, because of our sins against our own God. Therefore astounding things have happened.

[19] But do not think that you will go unpunished for having tried to fight against God!"

[20] The mother was especially admirable and worthy of honorable memory. Though she saw her seven sons perish within a single day, she bore it with good courage because of her hope in the Lord.

[21] She encouraged each of them in the language of their fathers. Filled with a noble spirit, she fired her woman's reasoning with a man's courage, and said to them,

[22] "I do not know how you came into being in my womb. It was not I who gave you life and breath, nor I who set in order the elements within each of you.

[23] Therefore the Creator of the world, who shaped the beginning of man and devised the origin of all things, will in his mercy give life and breath back to you again, since you now forget yourselves for the sake of his laws."

[24] Antiochus felt that he was being treated with contempt, and he was suspicious of her reproachful tone. The youngest brother being still alive, Antiochus not only appealed to him in words, but promised with oaths that he would make him rich and enviable if he would turn from the ways of his fathers, and that he would take him for his friend and entrust him with public affairs.

[25] Since the young man would not listen to him at all, the king called the mother to him and urged her to advise the youth to save himself.

[26] After much urging on his part, she undertook to persuade her son.

[27] But, leaning close to him, she spoke in their native tongue as follows, deriding the cruel tyrant: "My son, have pity on me. I carried you nine months in my womb, and nursed you for three years, and have reared you and brought you up to this point in your life, and have taken care of you.

[28] I beseech you, my child, to look at the heaven and the earth and see everything that is in them, and recognize that God did not make them out of things that existed. Thus also mankind comes into being.

[29] Do not fear this butcher, but prove worthy of your brothers. Accept death, so that in God's mercy I may get you back again with your brothers."

[30] While she was still speaking, the young man said, "What are you waiting for? I will not obey the king's command, but I obey the command of the law that was given to our fathers through Moses.

[31] But you, who have contrived all sorts of evil against the Hebrews, will certainly not escape the hands of God.

[32] For we are suffering because of our own sins.

[33] And if our living Lord is angry for a little while, to rebuke and discipline us, he will again be reconciled with his own servants.

[34] But you, unholy wretch, you most defiled of all men, do not be elated in vain and puffed up by uncertain hopes, when you raise your hand against the children of heaven.

[35] You have not yet escaped the judgment of the almighty, all-seeing God.

[36] For our brothers after enduring a brief suffering have drunk of everflowing life under God's covenant; but you, by the judgment of God, will receive just punishment for your arrogance.
[37] I, like my brothers, give up body and life for the laws of our fathers, appealing to God to show mercy soon to our nation and by afflictions and plagues to make you confess that he alone is God,
[38] and through me and my brothers to bring to an end the wrath of the Almighty which has justly fallen on our whole nation."
[39] The king fell into a rage, and handled him worse than the others, being exasperated at his scorn.
[40] So he died in his integrity, putting his whole trust in the Lord.
[41] Last of all, the mother died, after her sons.
[42] Let this be enough, then, about the eating of sacrifices and the extreme tortures.
2Mac.8
[1] But Judas, who was also called Maccabeus, and his companions secretly entered the villages and summoned their kinsmen and enlisted those who had continued in the Jewish faith, and so they gathered about six thousand men.
[2] They besought the Lord to look upon the people who were oppressed by all, and to have pity on the temple which had been profaned by ungodly men,
[3] and to have mercy on the city which was being destroyed and about to be leveled to the ground, and to hearken to the blood that cried out to him,
[4] and to remember also the lawless destruction of the innocent babies and the blasphemies committed against his name, and to show his hatred of evil.
[5] As soon as Maccabeus got his army organized, the Gentiles could not withstand him, for the wrath of the Lord had turned to mercy.
[6] Coming without warning, he would set fire to towns and villages. He captured strategic positions and put to flight not a few of the enemy.
[7] He found the nights most advantageous for such attacks. And talk of his valor spread everywhere.
[8] When Philip saw that the man was gaining ground little by little, and that he was pushing ahead with more frequent successes, he wrote to Ptolemy, the governor of Coelesyria and Phoenicia, for aid to the king's government.
[9] And Ptolemy promptly appointed Nicanor the son of Patroclus, one of the king's chief friends, and sent him, in command of no fewer than twenty thousand Gentiles of all nations, to wipe out the whole race of Judea. He associated with him Gorgias, a general and a man of experience in military service.
[10] Nicanor determined to make up for the king the tribute due to the Romans, two thousand talents, by selling the captured Jews into slavery.

[11] And he immediately sent to the cities on the seacoast, inviting them to buy Jewish slaves and promising to hand over ninety slaves for a talent, not expecting the judgment from the Almighty that was about to overtake him.

[12] Word came to Judas concerning Nicanor's invasion; and when he told his companions of the arrival of the army,

[13] those who were cowardly and distrustful of God's justice ran off and got away.

[14] Others sold all their remaining property, and at the same time besought the Lord to rescue those who had been sold by the ungodly Nicanor before he ever met them,

[15] if not for their own sake, yet for the sake of the covenants made with their fathers, and because he had called them by his holy and glorious name.

[16] But Maccabeus gathered his men together, to the number six thousand, and exhorted them not to be frightened by the enemy and not to fear the great multitude of Gentiles who were wickedly coming against them, but to fight nobly,

[17] keeping before their eyes the lawless outrage which the Gentiles had committed against the holy place, and the torture of the derided city, and besides, the overthrow of their ancestral way of life.

[18] "For they trust to arms and acts of daring," he said, "but we trust in the Almighty God, who is able with a single nod to strike down those who are coming against us and even the whole world."

[19] Moreover, he told them of the times when help came to their ancestors; both the time of Sennacherib, when one hundred and eighty-five thousand perished,

[20] and the time of the battle with the Galatians that took place in Babylonia, when eight thousand in all went into the affair, with four thousand Macedonians; and when the Macedonians were hard pressed, the eight thousand, by the help that came to them from heaven, destroyed one hundred and twenty thousand and took much booty.

[21] With these words he filled them with good courage and made them ready to die for their laws and their country; then he divided his army into four parts.

[22] He appointed his brothers also, Simon and Joseph and Jonathan, each to command a division, putting fifteen hundred men under each.

[23] Besides, he appointed Eleazar to read aloud from the holy book, and gave the watchword, "God's help"; then, leading the first division himself, he joined battle with Nicanor.

[24] With the Almighty as their ally, they slew more than nine thousand of the enemy, and wounded and disabled most of Nicanor's army, and forced them all to flee.

[25] They captured the money of those who had come to buy them as slaves. After pursuing them for some distance, they were obliged to return because the hour was late.

[26] For it was the day before the sabbath, and for that reason they did not continue their pursuit.

[27] And when they had collected the arms of the enemy and stripped them of their spoils, they kept the sabbath, giving great praise and thanks to the Lord, who had preserved them for that day and allotted it to them as the beginning of mercy.

[28] After the sabbath they gave some of the spoils to those who had been tortured and to the widows and orphans, and distributed the rest among themselves and their children.

[29] When they had done this, they made common supplication and besought the merciful Lord to be wholly reconciled with his servants.

[30] In encounters with the forces of Timothy and Bacchides they killed more than twenty thousand of them and got possession of some exceedingly high strongholds, and they divided very much plunder, giving to those who had been tortured and to the orphans and widows, and also to the aged, shares equal to their own.

[31] Collecting the arms of the enemy, they stored them all carefully in strategic places, and carried the rest of the spoils to Jerusalem.

[32] They killed the commander of Timothy's forces, a most unholy man, and one who had greatly troubled the Jews.

[33] While they were celebrating the victory in the city of their fathers, they burned those who had set fire to the sacred gates, Callisthenes and some others, who had fled into one little house; so these received the proper recompense for their impiety.

[34] The thrice-accursed Nicanor, who had brought the thousand merchants to buy the Jews,

[35] having been humbled with the help of the Lord by opponents whom he regarded as of the least account, took off his splendid uniform and made his way alone like a runaway slave across the country till he reached Antioch, having succeeded chiefly in the destruction of his own army!

[36] Thus he who had undertaken to secure tribute for the Romans by the capture of the people of Jerusalem proclaimed that the Jews had a Defender, and that therefore the Jews were invulnerable, because they followed the laws ordained by him.

2Mac.9

[1] About that time, as it happened, Antiochus had retreated in disorder from the region of Persia.

[2] For he had entered the city called Persepolis, and attempted to rob the temples and control the city. Therefore the people rushed to the rescue with arms, and Antiochus and his men were defeated, with the result that Antiochus was put to flight by the inhabitants and beat a shameful retreat.

[3] While he was in Ecbatana, news came to him of what had happened to Nicanor and the forces of Timothy.

[4] Transported with rage, he conceived the idea of turning upon the Jews the injury done by those who had put him to flight; so he ordered his charioteer to drive without stopping until he completed the journey. But the judgment of heaven rode with him! For in his arrogance he said, "When I get there I will make Jerusalem a cemetery of Jews."

[5] But the all-seeing Lord, the God of Israel, struck him an incurable and unseen blow. As soon as he ceased speaking he was seized with a pain in his bowels for which there was no relief and with sharp internal tortures --

[6] and that very justly, for he had tortured the bowels of others with many and strange inflictions.

[7] Yet he did not in any way stop his insolence, but was even more filled with arrogance, breathing fire in his rage against the Jews, and giving orders to hasten the journey. And so it came about that he fell out of his chariot as it was rushing along, and the fall was so hard as to torture every limb of his body.

[8] Thus he who had just been thinking that he could command the waves of the sea, in his superhuman arrogance, and imagining that he could weigh the high mountains in a balance, was brought down to earth and carried in a litter, making the power of God manifest to all.

[9] And so the ungodly man's body swarmed with worms, and while he was still living in anguish and pain, his flesh rotted away, and because of his stench the whole army felt revulsion at his decay.

[10] Because of his intolerable stench no one was able to carry the man who a little while before had thought that he could touch the stars of heaven.

[11] Then it was that, broken in spirit, he began to lose much of his arrogance and to come to his senses under the scourge of God, for he was tortured with pain every moment.

[12] And when he could not endure his own stench, he uttered these words: "It is right to be subject to God, and no mortal should think that he is equal to God."

[13] Then the abominable fellow made a vow to the Lord, who would no longer have mercy on him, stating

[14] that the holy city, which he was hastening to level to the ground and to make a cemetery, he was now declaring to be free;

[15] and the Jews, whom he had not considered worth burying but had planned to throw out with their children to the beasts, for the birds to pick, he would make, all of them, equal to citizens of Athens;

[16] and the holy sanctuary, which he had formerly plundered, he would adorn with the finest offerings; and the holy vessels he would give back, all of them, many times over; and the expenses incurred for the sacrifices he would provide from his own revenues;

[17] and in addition to all this he also would become a Jew and would visit every inhabited place to proclaim the power of God.

[18] But when his sufferings did not in any way abate, for the judgment of God had justly come upon him, he gave up all hope for himself and wrote to the Jews the following letter, in the form of a supplication. This was its content:

[19] "To his worthy Jewish citizens, Antiochus their king and general sends hearty greetings and good wishes for their health and prosperity.

[20] If you and your children are well and your affairs are as you wish, I am glad. As my hope is in heaven,

[21] I remember with affection your esteem and good will. On my way back from the region of Persia I suffered an annoying illness, and I have deemed it necessary to take thought for the general security of all.

[22] I do not despair of my condition, for I have good hope of recovering from my illness,

[23] but I observed that my father, on the occasions when he made expeditions into the upper country, appointed his successor,

[24] so that, if anything unexpected happened or any unwelcome news came, the people throughout the realm would not be troubled, for they would know to whom the government was left.

[25] Moreover, I understand how the princes along the borders and the neighbors to my kingdom keep watching for opportunities and waiting to see what will happen. So I have appointed my son Antiochus to be king, whom I have often entrusted and commended to most of you when I hastened off to the upper provinces; and I have written to him what is written here.

[26] I therefore urge and beseech you to remember the public and private services rendered to you and to maintain your present good will, each of you, toward me and my son.

[27] For I am sure that he will follow my policy and will treat you with moderation and kindness."

[28] So the murderer and blasphemer, having endured the more intense suffering, such as he had inflicted on others, came to the end of his life by a most pitiable fate, among the mountains in a strange land.

[29] And Philip, one of his courtiers, took his body home; then, fearing the son of Antiochus, he betook himself to Ptolemy Philometor in Egypt. 2Mac.10

[1] Now Maccabeus and his followers, the Lord leading them on, recovered the temple and the city;

[2] and they tore down the altars which had been built in the public square by the foreigners, and also destroyed the sacred precincts.

[3] They purified the sanctuary, and made another altar of sacrifice; then, striking fire out of flint, they offered sacrifices, after a lapse of two years,

and they burned incense and lighted lamps and set out the bread of the Presence.

[4] And when they had done this, they fell prostrate and besought the Lord that they might never again fall into such misfortunes, but that, if they should ever sin, they might be disciplined by him with forbearance and not be handed over to blasphemous and barbarous nations.

[5] It happened that on the same day on which the sanctuary had been profaned by the foreigners, the purification of the sanctuary took place, that is, on the twenty-fifth day of the same month, which was Chislev.

[6] And they celebrated it for eight days with rejoicing, in the manner of the feast of booths, remembering how not long before, during the feast of booths, they had been wandering in the mountains and caves like wild animals.

[7] Therefore bearing ivy-wreathed wands and beautiful branches and also fronds of palm, they offered hymns of thanksgiving to him who had given success to the purifying of his own holy place.

[8] They decreed by public ordinance and vote that the whole nation of the Jews should observe these days every year.

[9] Such then was the end of Antiochus, who was called Epiphanes.

[10] Now we will tell what took place under Antiochus Eupator, who was the son of that ungodly man, and will give a brief summary of the principal calamities of the wars.

[11] This man, when he succeeded to the kingdom, appointed one Lysias to have charge of the government and to be chief governor of Coelesyria and Phoenicia.

[12] Ptolemy, who was called Macron, took the lead in showing justice to the Jews because of the wrong that had been done to them, and attempted to maintain peaceful relations with them.

[13] As a result he was accused before Eupator by the king's friends. He heard himself called a traitor at every turn, because he had abandoned Cyprus, which Philometor had entrusted to him, and had gone over to Antiochus Epiphanes. Unable to command the respect due his office, he took poison and ended his life.

[14] When Gorgias became governor of the region, he maintained a force of mercenaries, and at every turn kept on warring against the Jews.

[15] Besides this, the Idumeans, who had control of important strongholds, were harassing the Jews; they received those who were banished from Jerusalem, and endeavored to keep up the war.

[16] But Maccabeus and his men, after making solemn supplication and beseeching God to fight on their side, rushed to the strongholds of the Idumeans.

[17] Attacking them vigorously, they gained possession of the places, and beat off all who fought upon the wall, and slew those whom they encountered, killing no fewer than twenty thousand.

[18] When no less than nine thousand took refuge in two very strong towers well equipped to withstand a siege,

[19] Maccabeus left Simon and Joseph, and also Zacchaeus and his men, a force sufficient to besiege them; and he himself set off for places where he was more urgently needed.

[20] But the men with Simon, who were money-hungry, were bribed by some of those who were in the towers, and on receiving seventy thousand drachmas let some of them slip away.

[21] When word of what had happened came to Maccabeus, he gathered the leaders of the people, and accused these men of having sold their brethren for money by setting their enemies free to fight against them.

[22] Then he slew these men who had turned traitor, and immediately captured the two towers.

[23] Having success at arms in everything he undertook, he destroyed more than twenty thousand in the two strongholds.

[24] Now Timothy, who had been defeated by the Jews before, gathered a tremendous force of mercenaries and collected the cavalry from Asia in no small number. He came on, intending to take Judea by storm.

[25] As he drew near, Maccabeus and his men sprinkled dust upon their heads and girded their loins with sackcloth, in supplication to God.

[26] Falling upon the steps before the altar, they besought him to be gracious to them and to be an enemy to their enemies and an adversary to their adversaries, as the law declares.

[27] And rising from their prayer they took up their arms and advanced a considerable distance from the city; and when they came near to the enemy they halted.

[28] Just as dawn was breaking, the two armies joined battle, the one having as pledge of success and victory not only their valor but their reliance upon the Lord, while the other made rage their leader in the fight.

[29] When the battle became fierce, there appeared to the enemy from heaven five resplendent men on horses with golden bridles, and they were leading the Jews.

[30] Surrounding Maccabeus and protecting him with their own armor and weapons, they kept him from being wounded. And they showered arrows and thunderbolts upon the enemy, so that, confused and blinded, they were thrown into disorder and cut to pieces.

[31] Twenty thousand five hundred were slaughtered, besides six hundred horsemen.

[32] Timothy himself fled to a stronghold called Gazara, especially well garrisoned, where Chaereas was commander.

[33] Then Maccabeus and his men were glad, and they besieged the fort for four days.

[34] The men within, relying on the strength of the place, blasphemed terribly and hurled out wicked words.

[35] But at dawn of the fifth day, twenty young men in the army of Maccabeus, fired with anger because of the blasphemies, bravely stormed the wall and with savage fury cut down every one they met.

[36] Others who came up in the same way wheeled around against the defenders and set fire to the towers; they kindled fires and burned the blasphemers alive. Others broke open the gates and let in the rest of the force, and they occupied the city.

[37] They killed Timothy, who was hidden in a cistern, and his brother Chaereas, and Apollophanes.

[38] When they had accomplished these things, with hymns and thanksgivings they blessed the Lord who shows great kindness to Israel and gives them the victory.

2Mac.11

[1] Very soon after this, Lysias, the king's guardian and kinsman, who was in charge of the government, being vexed at what had happened,

[2] gathered about eighty thousand men and all his cavalry and came against the Jews. He intended to make the city a home for Greeks,

[3] and to levy tribute on the temple as he did on the sacred places of the other nations, and to put up the high priesthood for sale every year.

[4] He took no account whatever of the power of God, but was elated with his ten thousands of infantry, and his thousands of cavalry, and his eighty elephants.

[5] Invading Judea, he approached Beth-zur, which was a fortified place about five leagues from Jerusalem, and pressed it hard.

[6] When Maccabeus and his men got word that Lysias was besieging the strongholds, they and all the people, with lamentations and tears, besought the Lord to send a good angel to save Israel.

[7] Maccabeus himself was the first to take up arms, and he urged the others to risk their lives with him to aid their brethren. Then they eagerly rushed off together.

[8] And there, while they were still near Jerusalem, a horseman appeared at their head, clothed in white and brandishing weapons of gold.

[9] And they all together praised the merciful God, and were strengthened in heart, ready to assail not only men but the wildest beasts or walls of iron.

[10] They advanced in battle order, having their heavenly ally, for the Lord had mercy on them.

[11] They hurled themselves like lions against the enemy, and slew eleven thousand of them and sixteen hundred horsemen, and forced all the rest to flee.

[12] Most of them got away stripped and wounded, and Lysias himself escaped by disgraceful flight.

[13] And as he was not without intelligence, he pondered over the defeat which had befallen him, and realized that the Hebrews were invincible because the mighty God fought on their side. So he sent to them

[14] and persuaded them to settle everything on just terms, promising that he would persuade the king, constraining him to be their friend.

[15] Maccabeus, having regard for the common good, agreed to all that Lysias urged. For the king granted every request in behalf of the Jews which Maccabeus delivered to Lysias in writing.

[16] The letter written to the Jews by Lysias was to this effect: "Lysias to the people of the Jews, greeting.

[17] John and Absalom, who were sent by you, have delivered your signed communication and have asked about the matters indicated therein.

[18] I have informed the king of everything that needed to be brought before him, and he has agreed to what was possible.

[19] If you will maintain your good will toward the government, I will endeavor for the future to help promote your welfare.

[20] And concerning these matters and their details, I have ordered these men and my representatives to confer with you.

[21] Farewell. The one hundred and forty-eighth year, Dioscorinthius twenty-fourth."

[22] The king's letter ran thus: "King Antiochus to his brother Lysias, greeting.

[23] Now that our father has gone on to the gods, we desire that the subjects of the kingdom be undisturbed in caring for their own affairs.

[24] We have heard that the Jews do not consent to our father's change to Greek customs but prefer their own way of living and ask that their own customs be allowed them.

[25] Accordingly, since we choose that this nation also be free from disturbance, our decision is that their temple be restored to them and that they live according to the customs of their ancestors.

[26] You will do well, therefore, to send word to them and give them pledges of friendship, so that they may know our policy and be of good cheer and go on happily in the conduct of their own affairs."

[27] To the nation the king's letter was as follows: "King Antiochus to the senate of the Jews and to the other Jews, greeting.

[28] If you are well, it is as we desire. We also are in good health.

[29] Menelaus has informed us that you wish to return home and look after your own affairs.

[30] Therefore those who go home by the thirtieth day of Xanthicus will have our pledge of friendship and full permission

[31] for the Jews to enjoy their own food and laws, just as formerly, and none of them shall be molested in any way for what he may have done in ignorance.

[32] And I have also sent Menelaus to encourage you.

[33] Farewell. The one hundred and forty-eighth year, Xanthicus fifteenth."
[34] The Romans also sent them a letter, which read thus: "Quintus Memmius and Titus Manius, envoys of the Romans, to the people of the Jews, greeting.
[35] With regard to what Lysias the kinsman of the king has granted you, we also give consent.
[36] But as to the matters which he decided are to be referred to the king, as soon as you have considered them, send some one promptly, so that we may make proposals appropriate for you. For we are on our way to Antioch.
[37] Therefore make haste and send some men, so that we may have your judgment.
[38] Farewell. The one hundred and forty-eighth year, Xanthicus fifteenth."
2Mac.12
[1] When this agreement had been reached, Lysias returned to the king, and the Jews went about their farming.
[2] But some of the governors in various places, Timothy and Apollonius the son of Gennaeus, as well as Hieronymus and Demophon, and in addition to these Nicanor the governor of Cyprus, would not let them live quietly and in peace.
[3] And some men of Joppa did so ungodly a deed as this: they invited the Jews who lived among them to embark, with their wives and children, on boats which they had provided, as though there were no ill will to the Jews;
[4] and this was done by public vote of the city. And when they accepted, because they wished to live peaceably and suspected nothing, the men of Joppa took them out to sea and drowned them, not less than two hundred.
[5] When Judas heard of the cruelty visited on his countrymen, he gave orders to his men
[6] and, calling upon God the righteous Judge, attacked the murderers of his brethren. He set fire to the harbor by night, and burned the boats, and massacred those who had taken refuge there.
[7] Then, because the city's gates were closed, he withdrew, intending to come again and root out the whole community of Joppa.
[8] But learning that the men in Jamnia meant in the same way to wipe out the Jews who were living among them,
[9] he attacked the people of Jamnia by night and set fire to the harbor and the fleet, so that the glow of the light was seen in Jerusalem, thirty miles distant.
[10] When they had gone more than a mile from there, on their march against Timothy, not less than five thousand Arabs with five hundred horsemen attacked them.
[11] After a hard fight Judas and his men won the victory, by the help of God. The defeated nomads besought Judas to grant them pledges of

friendship, promising to give him cattle and to help his people in all other ways.

[12] Judas, thinking that they might really be useful in many ways, agreed to make peace with them; and after receiving his pledges they departed to their tents.

[13] He also attacked a certain city which was strongly fortified with earthworks and walls, and inhabited by all sorts of Gentiles. Its name was Caspin.

[14] And those who were within, relying on the strength of the walls and on their supply of provisions, behaved most insolently toward Judas and his men, railing at them and even blaspheming and saying unholy things.

[15] But Judas and his men, calling upon the great Sovereign of the world, who without battering-rams or engines of war overthrew Jericho in the days of Joshua, rushed furiously upon the walls.

[16] They took the city by the will of God, and slaughtered untold numbers, so that the adjoining lake, a quarter of a mile wide, appeared to be running over with blood.

[17] When they had gone ninety-five miles from there, they came to Charax, to the Jews who are called Toubiani.

[18] They did not find Timothy in that region, for he had by then departed from the region without accomplishing anything, though in one place he had left a very strong garrison.

[19] Dositheus and Sosipater, who were captains under Maccabeus, marched out and destroyed those whom Timothy had left in the stronghold, more than ten thousand men.

[20] But Maccabeus arranged his army in divisions, set men in command of the divisions, and hastened after Timothy, who had with him a hundred and twenty thousand infantry and two thousand five hundred cavalry.

[21] When Timothy learned of the approach of Judas, he sent off the women and the children and also the baggage to a place called Carnaim; for that place was hard to besiege and difficult of access because of the narrowness of all the approaches.

[22] But when Judas' first division appeared, terror and fear came over the enemy at the manifestation to them of him who sees all things; and they rushed off in flight and were swept on, this way and that, so that often they were injured by their own men and pierced by the points of their swords.

[23] And Judas pressed the pursuit with the utmost vigor, putting the sinners to the sword, and destroyed as many as thirty thousand men.

[24] Timothy himself fell into the hands of Dositheus and Sosipater and their men. With great guile he besought them to let him go in safety, because he held the parents of most of them and the brothers of some and no consideration would be shown them.

[25] And when with many words he had confirmed his solemn promise to restore them unharmed, they let him go, for the sake of saving their brethren.

[26] Then Judas marched against Carnaim and the temple of Atargatis, and slaughtered twenty-five thousand people.

[27] After the rout and destruction of these, he marched also against Ephron, a fortified city where Lysias dwelt with multitudes of people of all nationalities. Stalwart young men took their stand before the walls and made a vigorous defense; and great stores of war engines and missiles were there.

[28] But the Jews called upon the Sovereign who with power shatters the might of his enemies, and they got the city into their hands, and killed as many as twenty-five thousand of those who were within it.

[29] Setting out from there, they hastened to Scythopolis, which is seventy-five miles from Jerusalem.

[30] But when the Jews who dwelt there bore witness to the good will which the people of Scythopolis had shown them and their kind treatment of them in times of misfortune,

[31] they thanked them and exhorted them to be well disposed to their race in the future also. Then they went up to Jerusalem, as the feast of weeks was close at hand.

[32] After the feast called Pentecost, they hastened against Gorgias, the governor of Idumea.

[33] And he came out with three thousand infantry and four hundred cavalry.

[34] When they joined battle, it happened that a few of the Jews fell.

[35] But a certain Dositheus, one of Bacenor's men, who was on horseback and was a strong man, caught hold of Gorgias, and grasping his cloak was dragging him off by main strength, wishing to take the accursed man alive, when one of the Thracian horsemen bore down upon him and cut off his arm; so Gorgias escaped and reached Marisa.

[36] As Esdris and his men had been fighting for a long time and were weary, Judas called upon the Lord to show himself their ally and leader in the battle.

[37] In the language of their fathers he raised the battle cry, with hymns; then he charged against Gorgias' men when they were not expecting it, and put them to flight.

[38] Then Judas assembled his army and went to the city of Adullam. As the seventh day was coming on, they purified themselves according to the custom, and they kept the sabbath there.

[39] On the next day, as by that time it had become necessary, Judas and his men went to take up the bodies of the fallen and to bring them back to lie with their kinsmen in the sepulchres of their fathers.

[40] Then under the tunic of every one of the dead they found sacred tokens of the idols of Jamnia, which the law forbids the Jews to wear. And it became clear to all that this was why these men had fallen.

[41] So they all blessed the ways of the Lord, the righteous Judge, who reveals the things that are hidden;

[42] and they turned to prayer, beseeching that the sin which had been committed might be wholly blotted out. And the noble Judas exhorted the people to keep themselves free from sin, for they had seen with their own eyes what had happened because of the sin of those who had fallen.

[43] He also took up a collection, man by man, to the amount of two thousand drachmas of silver, and sent it to Jerusalem to provide for a sin offering. In doing this he acted very well and honorably, taking account of the resurrection.

[44] For if he were not expecting that those who had fallen would rise again, it would have been superfluous and foolish to pray for the dead.

[45] But if he was looking to the splendid reward that is laid up for those who fall asleep in godliness, it was a holy and pious thought. Therefore he made atonement for the dead, that they might be delivered from their sin.

2Mac.13

[1] In the one hundred and forty-ninth year word came to Judas and his men that Antiochus Eupator was coming with a great army against Judea,

[2] and with him Lysias, his guardian, who had charge of the government. Each of them had a Greek force of one hundred and ten thousand infantry, five thousand three hundred cavalry, twenty-two elephants, and three hundred chariots armed with scythes.

[3] Menelaus also joined them and with utter hypocrisy urged Antiochus on, not for the sake of his country's welfare, but because he thought that he would be established in office.

[4] But the King of kings aroused the anger of Antiochus against the scoundrel; and when Lysias informed him that this man was to blame for all the trouble, he ordered them to take him to Beroea and to put him to death by the method which is the custom in that place.

[5] For there is a tower in that place, fifty cubits high, full of ashes, and it has a rim running around it which on all sides inclines precipitously into the ashes.

[6] There they all push to destruction any man guilty of sacrilege or notorious for other crimes.

[7] By such a fate it came about that Menelaus the lawbreaker died, without even burial in the earth.

[8] And this was eminently just; because he had committed many sins against the altar whose fire and ashes were holy, he met his death in ashes.

[9] The king with barbarous arrogance was coming to show the Jews things far worse than those that had been done in his father's time.

[10] But when Judas heard of this, he ordered the people to call upon the Lord day and night, now if ever to help those who were on the point of being deprived of the law and their country and the holy temple,

[11] and not to let the people who had just begun to revive fall into the hands of the blasphemous Gentiles.

[12] When they had all joined in the same petition and had besought the merciful Lord with weeping and fasting and lying prostrate for three days without ceasing, Judas exhorted them and ordered them to stand ready.

[13] After consulting privately with the elders, he determined to march out and decide the matter by the help of God before the king's army could enter Judea and get possession of the city.

[14] So, committing the decision to the Creator of the world and exhorting his men to fight nobly to the death for the laws, temple, city, country, and commonwealth, he pitched his camp near Modein.

[15] He gave his men the watchword, "God's victory," and with a picked force of the bravest young men, he attacked the king's pavilion at night and slew as many as two thousand men in the camp. He stabbed the leading elephant and its rider.

[16] In the end they filled the camp with terror and confusion and withdrew in triumph.

[17] This happened, just as day was dawning, because the Lord's help protected him.

[18] The king, having had a taste of the daring of the Jews, tried strategy in attacking their positions.

[19] He advanced against Beth-zur, a strong fortress of the Jews, was turned back, attacked again, and was defeated.

[20] Judas sent in to the garrison whatever was necessary.

[21] But Rhodocus, a man from the ranks of the Jews, gave secret information to the enemy; he was sought for, caught, and put in prison.

[22] The king negotiated a second time with the people in Beth-zur, gave pledges, received theirs, withdrew, attacked Judas and his men, was defeated;

[23] he got word that Philip, who had been left in charge of the government, had revolted in Antioch; he was dismayed, called in the Jews, yielded and swore to observe all their rights, settled with them and offered sacrifice, honored the sanctuary and showed generosity to the holy place.

[24] He received Maccabeus, left Hegemonides as governor from Ptolemais to Gerar,

[25] and went to Ptolemais. The people of Ptolemais were indignant over the treaty; in fact they were so angry that they wanted to annul its terms.

[26] Lysias took the public platform, made the best possible defense, convinced them, appeased them, gained their good will, and set out for Antioch. This is how the king's attack and withdrawal turned out.
2Mac.14

[1] Three years later, word came to Judas and his men that Demetrius, the son of Seleucus, had sailed into the harbor of Tripolis with a strong army and a fleet,
[2] and had taken possession of the country, having made away with Antiochus and his guardian Lysias.
[3] Now a certain Alcimus, who had formerly been high priest but had wilfully defiled himself in the times of separation, realized that there was no way for him to be safe or to have access again to the holy altar,
[4] and went to King Demetrius in about the one hundred and fifty-first year, presenting to him a crown of gold and a palm, and besides these some of the customary olive branches from the temple. During that day he kept quiet.
[5] But he found an opportunity that furthered his mad purpose when he was invited by Demetrius to a meeting of the council and was asked about the disposition and intentions of the Jews. He answered:
[6] "Those of the Jews who are called Hasideans, whose leader is Judas Maccabeus, are keeping up war and stirring up sedition, and will not let the kingdom attain tranquillity.
[7] Therefore I have laid aside my ancestral glory -- I mean the high priesthood -- and have now come here,
[8] first because I am genuinely concerned for the interests of the king, and second because I have regard also for my fellow citizens. For through the folly of those whom I have mentioned our whole nation is now in no small misfortune.
[9] Since you are acquainted, O king, with the details of this matter, deign to take thought for our country and our hard-pressed nation with the gracious kindness which you show to all.
[10] For as long as Judas lives, it is impossible for the government to find peace."
[11] When he had said this, the rest of the king's friends, who were hostile to Judas, quickly inflamed Demetrius still more.
[12] And he immediately chose Nicanor, who had been in command of the elephants, appointed him governor of Judea, and sent him off
[13] with orders to kill Judas and scatter his men, and to set up Alcimus as high priest of the greatest temple.
[14] And the Gentiles throughout Judea, who had fled before Judas, flocked to join Nicanor, thinking that the misfortunes and calamities of the Jews would mean prosperity for themselves.
[15] When the Jews heard of Nicanor's coming and the gathering of the Gentiles, they sprinkled dust upon their heads and prayed to him who established his own people for ever and always upholds his own heritage by manifesting himself.
[16] At the command of the leader, they set out from there immediately and engaged them in battle at a village called Dessau.

[17] Simon, the brother of Judas, had encountered Nicanor, but had been temporarily checked because of the sudden consternation created by the enemy.

[18] Nevertheless Nicanor, hearing of the valor of Judas and his men and their courage in battle for their country, shrank from deciding the issue by bloodshed.

[19] Therefore he sent Posidonius and Theodotus and Mattathias to give and receive pledges of friendship.

[20] When the terms had been fully considered, and the leader had informed the people, and it had appeared that they were of one mind, they agreed to the covenant.

[21] And the leaders set a day on which to meet by themselves. A chariot came forward from each army; seats of honor were set in place;

[22] Judas posted armed men in readiness at key places to prevent sudden treachery on the part of the enemy; they held the proper conference.

[23] Nicanor stayed on in Jerusalem and did nothing out of the way, but dismissed the flocks of people that had gathered.

[24] And he kept Judas always in his presence; he was warmly attached to the man.

[25] And he urged him to marry and have children; so he married, settled down, and shared the common life.

[26] But when Alcimus noticed their good will for one another, he took the covenant that had been made and went to Demetrius. He told him that Nicanor was disloyal to the government, for he had appointed that conspirator against the kingdom, Judas, to be his successor.

[27] The king became excited and, provoked by the false accusations of that depraved man, wrote to Nicanor, stating that he was displeased with the covenant and commanding him to send Maccabeus to Antioch as a prisoner without delay.

[28] When this message came to Nicanor, he was troubled and grieved that he had to annul their agreement when the man had done no wrong.

[29] Since it was not possible to oppose the king, he watched for an opportunity to accomplish this by a stratagem.

[30] But Maccabeus, noticing that Nicanor was more austere in his dealings with him and was meeting him more rudely than had been his custom, concluded that this austerity did not spring from the best motives. So he gathered not a few of his men, and went into hiding from Nicanor.

[31] When the latter became aware that he had been cleverly outwitted by the man, he went to the great and holy temple while the priests were offering the customary sacrifices, and commanded them to hand the man over.

[32] And when they declared on oath that they did not know where the man was whom he sought,

[33] he stretched out his right hand toward the sanctuary, and swore this oath: "If you do not hand Judas over to me as a prisoner, I will level this precinct of God to the ground and tear down the altar, and I will build here a splendid temple to Dionysus."

[34] Having said this, he went away. Then the priests stretched forth their hands toward heaven and called upon the constant Defender of our nation, in these words:

[35] "O Lord of all, who hast need of nothing, thou wast pleased that there be a temple for thy habitation among us;

[36] so now, O holy One, Lord of all holiness, keep undefiled for ever this house that has been so recently purified."

[37] A certain Razis, one of the elders of Jerusalem, was denounced to Nicanor as a man who loved his fellow citizens and was very well thought of and for his good will was called father of the Jews.

[38] For in former times, when there was no mingling with the Gentiles, he had been accused of Judaism, and for Judaism he had with all zeal risked body and life.

[39] Nicanor, wishing to exhibit the enmity which he had for the Jews, sent more than five hundred soldiers to arrest him;

[40] for he thought that by arresting him he would do them an injury.

[41] When the troops were about to capture the tower and were forcing the door of the courtyard, they ordered that fire be brought and the doors burned. Being surrounded, Razis fell upon his own sword,

[42] preferring to die nobly rather than to fall into the hands of sinners and suffer outrages unworthy of his noble birth.

[43] But in the heat of the struggle he did not hit exactly, and the crowd was now rushing in through the doors. He bravely ran up on the wall, and manfully threw himself down into the crowd.

[44] But as they quickly drew back, a space opened and he fell in the middle of the empty space.

[45] Still alive and aflame with anger, he rose, and though his blood gushed forth and his wounds were severe he ran through the crowd; and standing upon a steep rock,

[46] with his blood now completely drained from him, he tore out his entrails, took them with both hands and hurled them at the crowd, calling upon the Lord of life and spirit to give them back to him again. This was the manner of his death.

2Mac.15

[1] When Nicanor heard that Judas and his men were in the region of Samaria, he made plans to attack them with complete safety on the day of rest.

[2] And when the Jews who were compelled to follow him said, "Do not destroy so savagely and barbarously, but show respect for the day which he who sees all things has honored and hallowed above other days,"

[3] the thrice-accursed wretch asked if there were a sovereign in heaven who had commanded the keeping of the sabbath day.

[4] And when they declared, "It is the living Lord himself, the Sovereign in heaven, who ordered us to observe the seventh day,"

[5] he replied, "And I am a sovereign also, on earth, and I command you to take up arms and finish the king's business." Nevertheless, he did not succeed in carrying out his abominable design.

[6] This Nicanor in his utter boastfulness and arrogance had determined to erect a public monument of victory over Judas and his men.

[7] But Maccabeus did not cease to trust with all confidence that he would get help from the Lord.

[8] And he exhorted his men not to fear the attack of the Gentiles, but to keep in mind the former times when help had come to them from heaven, and now to look for the victory which the Almighty would give them.

[9] Encouraging them from the law and the prophets, and reminding them also of the struggles they had won, he made them the more eager.

[10] And when he had aroused their courage, he gave his orders, at the same time pointing out the perfidy of the Gentiles and their violation of oaths.

[11] He armed each of them not so much with confidence in shields and spears as with the inspiration of brave words, and he cheered them all by relating a dream, a sort of vision, which was worthy of belief.

[12] What he saw was this: Onias, who had been high priest, a noble and good man, of modest bearing and gentle manner, one who spoke fittingly and had been trained from childhood in all that belongs to excellence, was praying with outstretched hands for the whole body of the Jews.

[13] Then likewise a man appeared, distinguished by his gray hair and dignity, and of marvelous majesty and authority.

[14] And Onias spoke, saying, "This is a man who loves the brethren and prays much for the people and the holy city, Jeremiah, the prophet of God."

[15] Jeremiah stretched out his right hand and gave to Judas a golden sword, and as he gave it he addressed him thus:

[16] "Take this holy sword, a gift from God, with which you will strike down your adversaries."

[17] Encouraged by the words of Judas, so noble and so effective in arousing valor and awaking manliness in the souls of the young, they determined not to carry on a campaign but to attack bravely, and to decide the matter, by fighting hand to hand with all courage, because the city and the sanctuary and the temple were in danger.

[18] Their concern for wives and children, and also for brethren and relatives, lay upon them less heavily; their greatest and first fear was for the consecrated sanctuary.

[19] And those who had to remain in the city were in no little distress, being anxious over the encounter in the open country.
[20] When all were now looking forward to the coming decision, and the enemy was already close at hand with their army drawn up for battle, the elephants strategically stationed and the cavalry deployed on the flanks,
[21] Maccabeus, perceiving the hosts that were before him and the varied supply of arms and the savagery of the elephants, stretched out his hands toward heaven and called upon the Lord who works wonders; for he knew that it is not by arms, but as the Lord decides, that he gains the victory for those who deserve it.
[22] And he called upon him in these words: "O Lord, thou didst send thy angel in the time of Hezekiah king of Judea, and he slew fully a hundred and eighty-five thousand in the camp of Sennacherib.
[23] So now, O Sovereign of the heavens, send a good angel to carry terror and trembling before us.
[24] By the might of thy arm may these blasphemers who come against thy holy people be struck down." With these words he ended his prayer.
[25] Nicanor and his men advanced with trumpets and battle songs;
[26] and Judas and his men met the enemy in battle with invocation to God and prayers.
[27] So, fighting with their hands and praying to God in their hearts, they laid low no less than thirty-five thousand men, and were greatly gladdened by God's manifestation.
[28] When the action was over and they were returning with joy, they recognized Nicanor, lying dead, in full armor.
[29] Then there was shouting and tumult, and they blessed the Sovereign Lord in the language of their fathers.
[30] And the man who was ever in body and soul the defender of his fellow citizens, the man who maintained his youthful good will toward his countrymen, ordered them to cut off Nicanor's head and arm and carry them to Jerusalem.
[31] And when he arrived there and had called his countrymen together and stationed the priests before the altar, he sent for those who were in the citadel.
[32] He showed them the vile Nicanor's head and that profane man's arm, which had been boastfully stretched out against the holy house of the Almighty;
[33] and he cut out the tongue of the ungodly Nicanor and said that he would give it piecemeal to the birds and hang up these rewards of his folly opposite the sanctuary.
[34] And they all, looking to heaven, blessed the Lord who had manifested himself, saying, "Blessed is he who has kept his own place undefiled."
[35] And he hung Nicanor's head from the citadel, a clear and conspicuous sign to every one of the help of the Lord.

[36] And they all decreed by public vote never to let this day go unobserved, but to celebrate the thirteenth day of the twelfth month -- which is called Adar in the Syrian language -- the day before Mordecai's day.

[37] This, then, is how matters turned out with Nicanor. And from that time the city has been in the possession of the Hebrews. So I too will here end my story.

[38] If it is well told and to the point, that is what I myself desired; if it is poorly done and mediocre, that was the best I could do.

[39] For just as it is harmful to drink wine alone, or, again, to drink water alone, while wine mixed with water is sweet and delicious and enhances one's enjoyment, so also the style of the story delights the ears of those who read the work. And here will be the end.

3 Maccabees

3Mac.1

[1] When Philopator learned from those who returned that the regions which he had controlled had been seized by Antiochus, he gave orders to all his forces, both infantry and cavalry, took with him his sister Arsinoe, and marched out to the region near Raphia, where Antiochus's supporters were encamped.

[2] But a certain Theodotus, determined to carry out the plot he had devised, took with him the best of the Ptolemaic arms that had been previously issued to him, and crossed over by night to the tent of Ptolemy, intending single-handed to kill him and thereby end the war.

[3] But Dositheus, known as the son of Drimylus, a Jew by birth who later changed his religion and apostatized from the ancestral traditions, had led the king away and arranged that a certain insignificant man should sleep in the tent; and so it turned out that this man incurred the vengeance meant for the king.

[4] When a bitter fight resulted, and matters were turning out rather in favor of Antiochus, Arsinoe went to the troops with wailing and tears, her locks all disheveled, and exhorted them to defend themselves and their children and wives bravely, promising to give them each two minas of gold if they won the battle.

[5] And so it came about that the enemy was routed in the action, and many captives also were taken.

[6] Now that he had foiled the plot, Ptolemy decided to visit the neighboring cities and encourage them.

[7] By doing this, and by endowing their sacred enclosures with gifts, he strengthened the morale of his subjects.

[8] Since the Jews had sent some of their council and elders to greet him, to bring him gifts of welcome, and to congratulate him on what had happened, he was all the more eager to visit them as soon as possible.

[9] After he had arrived in Jerusalem, he offered sacrifice to the supreme God and made thank-offerings and did what was fitting for the holy place. Then, upon entering the place and being impressed by its excellence and its beauty,

[10] he marveled at the good order of the temple, and conceived a desire to enter the holy of holies.

[11] When they said that this was not permitted, because not even members of their own nation were allowed to enter, nor even all of the priests, but only the high priest who was pre-eminent over all, and he only once a year, the king was by no means persuaded.

[12] Even after the law had been read to him, he did not cease to maintain that he ought to enter, saying, "Even if those men are deprived of this honor, I ought not to be."

[13] And he inquired why, when he entered every other temple, no one there had stopped him.

[14] And someone heedlessly said that it was wrong to take this as a sign in itself.

[15] "But since this has happened," the king said, "why should not I at least enter, whether they wish it or not?"

[16] Then the priests in all their vestments prostrated themselves and entreated the supreme God to aid in the present situation and to avert the violence of this evil design, and they filled the temple with cries and tears;

[17] and those who remained behind in the city were agitated and hurried out, supposing that something mysterious was occurring.

[18] The virgins who had been enclosed in their chambers rushed out with their mothers, sprinkled their hair with dust, and filled the streets with groans and lamentations.

[19] Those women who had recently been arrayed for marriage abandoned the bridal chambers prepared for wedded union, and, neglecting proper modesty, in a disorderly rush flocked together in the city.

[20] Mothers and nurses abandoned even newborn children here and there, some in houses and some in the streets, and without a backward look they crowded together at the most high temple.

[21] Various were the supplications of those gathered there because of what the king was profanely plotting.

[22] In addition, the bolder of the citizens would not tolerate the completion of his plans or the fulfillment of his intended purpose.

[23] They shouted to their fellows to take arms and die courageously for the ancestral law, and created a considerable disturbance in the holy place; and being barely restrained by the old men and the elders, they resorted to the same posture of supplication as the others.

[24] Meanwhile the crowd, as before, was engaged in prayer,

[25] while the elders near the king tried in various ways to change his arrogant mind from the plan that he had conceived.

[26] But he, in his arrogance, took heed of nothing, and began now to approach, determined to bring the aforesaid plan to a conclusion.

[27] When those who were around him observed this, they turned, together with our people, to call upon him who has all power to defend them in the present trouble and not to overlook this unlawful and haughty deed.

[28] The continuous, vehement, and concerted cry of the crowds resulted in an immense uproar;

[29] for it seemed that not only the men but also the walls and the whole earth around echoed, because indeed all at that time preferred death to the profanation of the place.

3Mac.2

[1] Then the high priest Simon, facing the sanctuary, bending his knees and extending his hands with calm dignity, prayed as follows:

[2] "Lord, Lord, king of the heavens, and sovereign of all creation, holy among the holy ones, the only ruler, almighty, give attention to us who are suffering grievously from an impious and profane man, puffed up in his audacity and power.

[3] For you, the creator of all things and the governor of all, are a just Ruler, and you judge those who have done anything in insolence and arrogance.

[4] You destroyed those who in the past committed injustice, among whom were even giants who trusted in their strength and boldness, whom you destroyed by bringing upon them a boundless flood.

[5] You consumed with fire and sulphur the men of Sodom who acted arrogantly, who were notorious for their vices; and you made them an example to those who should come afterward.

[6] You made known your mighty power by inflicting many and varied punishments on the audacious Pharaoh who had enslaved your holy people Israel.

[7] And when he pursued them with chariots and a mass of troops, you overwhelmed him in the depths of the sea, but carried through safely those who had put their confidence in you, the Ruler over the whole creation.

[8] And when they had seen works of your hands, they praised you, the Almighty.

[9] You, O King, when you had created the boundless and immeasurable earth, chose this city and sanctified this place for your name, though you have no need of anything; and when you had glorified it by your magnificent manifestation, you made it a firm foundation for the glory of your great and honored name.

[10] And because you love the house of Israel, you promised that if we should have reverses, and tribulation should overtake us, you would listen to our petition when we come to this place and pray.

[11] And indeed you are faithful and true.

[12] And because oftentimes when our fathers were oppressed you helped them in their humiliation, and rescued them from great evils,

[13] see now, O holy King, that because of our many and great sins we are crushed with suffering, subjected to our enemies, and overtaken by helplessness.

[14] In our downfall this audacious and profane man undertakes to violate the holy place on earth dedicated to your glorious name.

[15] For your dwelling, the heaven of heavens, is unapproachable by man.

[16] But because you graciously bestowed your glory upon your people Israel, you sanctified this place.

[17] Do not punish us for the defilement committed by these men, or call us to account for this profanation, lest the transgressors boast in their wrath or exult in the arrogance of their tongue, saying,

[18] `We have trampled down the house of the sanctuary as offensive houses are trampled down.'

[19] Wipe away our sins and disperse our errors, and reveal your mercy at this hour.

[20] Speedily let your mercies overtake us, and put praises in the mouth of those who are downcast and broken in spirit, and give us peace."

[21] Thereupon God, who oversees all things, the first Father of all, holy among the holy ones, having heard the lawful supplication, scourged him who had exalted himself in insolence and audacity.

[22] He shook him on this side and that as a reed is shaken by the wind, so that he lay helpless on the ground and, besides being paralyzed in his limbs, was unable even to speak, since he was smitten by a righteous judgment.

[23] Then both friends and bodyguards, seeing the severe punishment that had overtaken him, and fearing lest he should lose his life, quickly dragged him out, panic-stricken in their exceedingly great fear.

[24] After a while he recovered, and though he had been punished, he by no means repented, but went away uttering bitter threats.

[25] When he arrived in Egypt, he increased in his deeds of malice, abetted by the previously mentioned drinking companions and comrades, who were strangers to everything just.

[26] He was not content with his uncounted licentious deeds, but he also continued with such audacity that he framed evil reports in the various localities; and many of his friends, intently observing the king's purpose, themselves also followed his will.

[27] He proposed to inflict public disgrace upon the Jewish community, and he set up a stone on the tower in the courtyard with this inscription:

[28] "None of those who do not sacrifice shall enter their sanctuaries, and all Jews shall be subjected to a registration involving poll tax and to the status of slaves. Those who object to this are to be taken by force and put to death;

[29] those who are registered are also to be branded on their bodies by fire with the ivy-leaf symbol of Dionysus, and they shall also be reduced to their former limited status."

[30] In order that he might not appear to be an enemy to all, he inscribed below: "But if any of them prefer to join those who have been initiated into the mysteries, they shall have equal citizenship with the Alexandrians."

[31] Now some, however, with an obvious abhorrence of the price to be exacted for maintaining the religion of their city, readily gave themselves

up, since they expected to enhance their reputation by their future association with the king.

[32] But the majority acted firmly with a courageous spirit and did not depart from their religion; and by paying money in exchange for life they confidently attempted to save themselves from the registration.

[33] They remained resolutely hopeful of obtaining help, and they abhorred those who separated themselves from them, considering them to be enemies of the Jewish nation, and depriving them of common fellowship and mutual help.

3Mac.3

[1] When the impious king comprehended this situation, he became so infuriated that not only was he enraged against those Jews who lived in Alexandria, but was still more bitterly hostile toward those in the countryside; and he ordered that all should promptly be gathered into one place, and put to death by the most cruel means.

[2] While these matters were being arranged, a hostile rumor was circulated against the Jewish nation by men who conspired to do them ill, a pretext being given by a report that they hindered others from the observance of their customs.

[3] The Jews, however, continued to maintain good will and unswerving loyalty toward the dynasty;

[4] but because they worshiped God and conducted themselves by his law, they kept their separateness with respect to foods. For this reason they appeared hateful to some;

[5] but since they adorned their style of life with the good deeds of upright people, they were established in good repute among all men.

[6] Nevertheless those of other races paid no heed to their good service to their nation, which was common talk among all;

[7] instead they gossiped about the differences in worship and foods, alleging that these people were loyal neither to the king nor to his authorities, but were hostile and greatly opposed to his government. So they attached no ordinary reproach to them.

[8] The Greeks in the city, though wronged in no way, when they saw an unexpected tumult around these people and the crowds that suddenly were forming, were not strong enough to help them, for they lived under tyranny. They did try to console them, being grieved at the situation, and expected that matters would change;

[9] for such a great community ought not be left to its fate when it had committed no offense.

[10] And already some of their neighbors and friends and business associates had taken some of them aside privately and were pledging to protect them and to exert more earnest efforts for their assistance.

[11] Then the king, boastful of his present good fortune, and not considering the might of the supreme God, but assuming that he would persevere constantly in his same purpose, wrote this letter against them:

[12] "King Ptolemy Philopator to his generals and soldiers in Egypt and all its districts, greetings and good health.

[13] I myself and our government are faring well.

[14] When our expedition took place in Asia, as you yourselves know, it was brought to conclusion, according to plan, by the gods' deliberate alliance with us in battle,

[15] and we considered that we should not rule the nations inhabiting Coele-Syria and Phoenicia by the power of the spear but should cherish them with clemency and great benevolence, gladly treating them well.

[16] And when we had granted very great revenues to the temples in the cities, we came on to Jerusalem also, and went up to honor the temple of those wicked people, who never cease from their folly.

[17] They accepted our presence by word, but insincerely by deed, because when we proposed to enter their inner temple and honor it with magnificent and most beautiful offerings,

[18] they were carried away by their traditional conceit, and excluded us from entering; but they were spared the exercise of our power because of the benevolence which we have toward all.

[19] By maintaining their manifest ill-will toward us, they become the only people among all nations who hold their heads high in defiance of kings and their own benefactors, and are unwilling to regard any action as sincere.

[20] "But we, when we arrived in Egypt victorious, accommodated ourselves to their folly and did as was proper, since we treat all nations with benevolence.

[21] Among other things, we made known to all our amnesty toward their compatriots here, both because of their alliance with us and the myriad affairs liberally entrusted to them from the beginning; and we ventured to make a change, by deciding both to deem them worthy of Alexandrian citizenship and to make them participants in our regular religious rites.

[22] But in their innate malice they took this in a contrary spirit, and disdained what is good. Since they incline constantly to evil,

[23] they not only spurn the priceless citizenship, but also both by speech and by silence they abominate those few among them who are sincerely disposed toward us; in every situation, in accordance with their infamous way of life, they secretly suspect that we may soon alter our policy.

[24] Therefore, fully convinced by these indications that they are ill-disposed toward us in every way, we have taken precautions lest, if a sudden disorder should later arise against us, we should have these impious people behind our backs as traitors and barbarous enemies.

[25] Therefore we have given orders that, as soon as this letter shall arrive, you are to send to us those who live among you, together with their wives and children, with insulting and harsh treatment, and bound securely with iron fetters, to suffer the sure and shameful death that befits enemies.
[26] For when these all have been punished, we are sure that for the remaining time the government will be established for ourselves in good order and in the best state.
[27] But whoever shelters any of the Jews, old people or children or even infants, will be tortured to death with the most hateful torments, together with his family.
[28] Any one willing to give information will receive the property of the one who incurs the punishment, and also two thousand drachmas from the royal treasury, and will be awarded his freedom.
[29] Every place detected sheltering a Jew is to be made unapproachable and burned with fire, and shall become useless for all time to any mortal creature."
[30] The letter was written in the above form.
3Mac.4
[1] In every place, then, where this decree arrived, a feast at public expense was arranged for the Gentiles with shouts and gladness, for the inveterate enmity which had long ago been in their minds was now made evident and outspoken.
[2] But among the Jews there was incessant mourning, lamentation, and tearful cries; everywhere their hearts were burning, and they groaned because of the unexpected destruction that had suddenly been decreed for them.
[3] What district or city, or what habitable place at all, or what streets were not filled with mourning and wailing for them?
[4] For with such a harsh and ruthless spirit were they being sent off, all together, by the generals in the several cities, that at the sight of their unusual punishments, even some of their enemies, perceiving the common object of pity before their eyes, reflected upon the uncertainty of life and shed tears at the most miserable expulsion of these people.
[5] For a multitude of gray-headed old men, sluggish and bent with age, was being led away, forced to march at a swift pace by the violence with which they were driven in such a shameful manner.
[6] And young women who had just entered the bridal chamber to share married life exchanged joy for wailing, their myrrh-perfumed hair sprinkled with ashes, and were carried away unveiled, all together raising a lament instead of a wedding song, as they were torn by the harsh treatment of the heathen.
[7] In bonds and in public view they were violently dragged along as far as the place of embarkation.

[8] Their husbands, in the prime of youth, their necks encircled with ropes instead of garlands, spent the remaining days of their marriage festival in lamentations instead of good cheer and youthful revelry, seeing death immediately before them.

[9] They were brought on board like wild animals, driven under the constraint of iron bonds; some were fastened by the neck to the benches of the boats, others had their feet secured by unbreakable fetters,

[10] and in addition they were confined under a solid deck, so that with their eyes in total darkness, they should undergo treatment befitting traitors during the whole voyage.

[11] When these men had been brought to the place called Schedia, and the voyage was concluded as the king had decreed, he commanded that they should be enclosed in the hippodrome which had been built with a monstrous perimeter wall in front of the city, and which was well suited to make them an obvious spectacle to all coming back into the city and to those from the city going out into the country, so that they could neither communicate with the king's forces nor in any way claim to be inside the circuit of the city.

[12] And when this had happened, the king, hearing that the Jews' compatriots from the city frequently went out in secret to lament bitterly the ignoble misfortune of their brothers,

[13] ordered in his rage that these men be dealt with in precisely the same fashion as the others, not omitting any detail of their punishment.

[14] The entire race was to be registered individually, not for the hard labor that has been briefly mentioned before, but to be tortured with the outrages that he had ordered, and at the end to be destroyed in the space of a single day.

[15] The registration of these people was therefore conducted with bitter haste and zealous intentness from the rising of the sun till its setting, and though uncompleted it stopped after forty days.

[16] The king was greatly and continually filled with joy, organizing feasts in honor of all his idols, with a mind alienated from truth and with a profane mouth, praising speechless things that are not able even to communicate or to come to one's help, and uttering improper words against the supreme God.

[17] But after the previously mentioned interval of time the scribes declared to the king that they were no longer able to take the census of the Jews because of their innumerable multitude,

[18] although most of them were still in the country, some still residing in their homes, and some at the place; the task was impossible for all the generals in Egypt.

[19] After he had threatened them severely, charging that they had been bribed to contrive a means of escape, he was clearly convinced about the matter

[20] when they said and proved that both the paper and the pens they used for writing had already given out.

[21] But this was an act of the invincible providence of him who was aiding the Jews from heaven.

3Mac.5

[1] Then the king, completely inflexible, was filled with overpowering anger and wrath; so he summoned Hermon, keeper of the elephants,

[2] and ordered him on the following day to drug all the elephants -- five hundred in number -- with large handfuls of frankincense and plenty of unmixed wine, and to drive them in, maddened by the lavish abundance of liquor, so that the Jews might meet their doom.

[3] When he had given these orders he returned to his feasting, together with those of his friends and of the army who were especially hostile toward the Jews.

[4] And Hermon, keeper of the elephants, proceeded faithfully to carry out the orders.

[5] The servants in charge of the Jews went out in the evening and bound the hands of the wretched people and arranged for their continued custody through the night, convinced that the whole nation would experience its final destruction.

[6] For to the Gentiles it appeared that the Jews were left without any aid,

[7] because in their bonds they were forcibly confined on every side. But with tears and a voice hard to silence they all called upon the Almighty Lord and Ruler of all power, their merciful God and Father, praying

[8] that he avert with vengeance the evil plot against them and in a glorious manifestation rescue them from the fate now prepared for them.

[9] So their entreaty ascended fervently to heaven.

[10] Hermon, however, when he had drugged the pitiless elephants until they had been filled with a great abundance of wine and satiated with frankincense, presented himself at the courtyard early in the morning to report to the king about these preparations.

[11] But the Lord sent upon the king a portion of sleep, that beneficence which from the beginning, night and day, is bestowed by him who grants it to whomever he wishes.

[12] And by the action of the Lord he was overcome by so pleasant and deep a sleep that he quite failed in his lawless purpose and was completely frustrated in his inflexible plan.

[13] Then the Jews, since they had escaped the appointed hour, praised their holy God and again begged him who is easily reconciled to show the might of his all-powerful hand to the arrogant Gentiles.

[14] But now, since it was nearly the middle of the tenth hour, the person who was in charge of the invitations, seeing that the guests were assembled, approached the king and nudged him.

[15] And when he had with difficulty roused him, he pointed out that the hour of the banquet was already slipping by, and he gave him an account of the situation.

[16] The king, after considering this, returned to his drinking, and ordered those present for the banquet to recline opposite him.

[17] When this was done he urged them to give themselves over to revelry and to make the present portion of the banquet joyful by celebrating all the more.

[18] After the party had been going on for some time, the king summoned Hermon and with sharp threats demanded to know why the Jews had been allowed to remain alive through the present day.

[19] But when he, with the corroboration of his friends, pointed out that while it was still night he had carried out completely the order given him,

[20] the king, possessed by a savagery worse than that of Phalaris, said that the Jews were benefited by today's sleep, "but," he added, "tomorrow without delay prepare the elephants in the same way for the destruction of the lawless Jews!"

[21] When the king had spoken, all those present readily and joyfully with one accord gave their approval, and each departed to his own home.

[22] But they did not so much employ the duration of the night in sleep as in devising all sorts of insults for those they thought to be doomed.

[23] Then, as soon as the cock had crowed in the early morning, Hermon, having equipped the beasts, began to move them along in the great colonnade.

[24] The crowds of the city had been assembled for this most pitiful spectacle and they were eagerly waiting for daybreak.

[25] But the Jews, at their last gasp, since the time had run out, stretched their hands toward heaven and with most tearful supplication and mournful dirges implored the supreme God to help them again at once.

[26] The rays of the sun were not yet shed abroad, and while the king was receiving his friends, Hermon arrived and invited him to come out, indicating that what the king desired was ready for action.

[27] But he, upon receiving the report and being struck by the unusual invitation to come out -- since he had been completely overcome by incomprehension -- inquired what the matter was for which this had been so zealously completed for him.

[28] This was the act of God who rules over all things, for he had implanted in the king's mind a forgetfulness of the things he had previously devised.

[29] Then Hermon and all the king's friends pointed out that the beasts and the armed forces were ready, "O king, according to your eager purpose."

[30] But at these words he was filled with an overpowering wrath, because by the providence of God his whole mind had been deranged in regard to these matters; and with a threatening look he said,

[31] "Were your parents or children present, I would have prepared them to be a rich feast for the savage beasts instead of the Jews, who give me no ground for complaint and have exhibited to an extraordinary degree a full and firm loyalty to my ancestors.

[32] In fact you would have been deprived of life instead of these, were it not for an affection arising from our nurture in common and your usefulness."

[33] So Hermon suffered an unexpected and dangerous threat, and his eyes wavered and his face fell.

[34] The king's friends one by one sullenly slipped away and dismissed the assembled people, each to his own occupation.

[35] Then the Jews, upon hearing what the king had said, praised the manifest Lord God, King of kings, since this also was his aid which they had received.

[36] The king, however, reconvened the party in the same manner and urged the guests to return to their celebrating.

[37] After summoning Hermon he said in a threatening tone, "How many times, you poor wretch, must I give you orders about these things?

[38] Equip the elephants now once more for the destruction of the Jews tomorrow!"

[39] But the officials who were at table with him, wondering at his instability of mind, remonstrated as follows:

[40] "O king, how long will you try us, as though we are idiots, ordering now for a third time that they be destroyed, and again revoking your decree in the matter?

[41] As a result the city is in a tumult because of its expectation; it is crowded with masses of people, and also in constant danger of being plundered."

[42] Upon this the king, a Phalaris in everything and filled with madness, took no account of the changes of mind which had come about within him for the protection of the Jews, and he firmly swore an irrevocable oath that he would send them to death without delay, mangled by the knees and feet of the beasts,

[43] and would also march against Judea and rapidly level it to the ground with fire and spear, and by burning to the ground the temple inaccessible to him would quickly render it forever empty of those who offered sacrifices there.

[44] Then the friends and officers departed with great joy, and they confidently posted the armed forces at the places in the city most favorable for keeping guard.

[45] Now when the beasts had been brought virtually to a state of madness, so to speak, by the very fragrant draughts of wine mixed with frankincense and had been equipped with frightful devices, the elephant keeper

[46] entered at about dawn into the courtyard -- the city now being filled with countless masses of people crowding their way into the hippodrome -- and urged the king on to the matter at hand.

[47] So he, when he had filled his impious mind with a deep rage, rushed out in full force along with the beasts, wishing to witness, with invulnerable heart and with his own eyes, the grievous and pitiful destruction of the aforementioned people.

[48] And when the Jews saw the dust raised by the elephants going out at the gate and by the following armed forces, as well as by the trampling of the crowd, and heard the loud and tumultuous noise,

[49] they thought that this was their last moment of life, the end of their most miserable suspense, and giving way to lamentation and groans they kissed each other, embracing relatives and falling into one another's arms -- parents and children, mothers and daughters, and others with babies at their breasts who were drawing their last milk.

[50] Not only this, but when they considered the help which they had received before from heaven they prostrated themselves with one accord on the ground, removing the babies from their breasts,

[51] and cried out in a very loud voice, imploring the Ruler over every power to manifest himself and be merciful to them, as they stood now at the gates of death.

3Mac.6

[1] Then a certain Eleazar, famous among the priests of the country, who had attained a ripe old age and throughout his life had been adorned with every virtue, directed the elders around him to cease calling upon the holy God and prayed as follows:

[2] "King of great power, Almighty God Most High, governing all creation with mercy,

[3] look upon the descendants of Abraham, O Father, upon the children of the sainted Jacob, a people of your consecrated portion who are perishing as foreigners in a foreign land.

[4] Pharaoh with his abundance of chariots, the former ruler of this Egypt, exalted with lawless insolence and boastful tongue, you destroyed together with his arrogant army by drowning them in the sea, manifesting the light of your mercy upon the nation of Israel.

[5] Sennacherib exulting in his countless forces, oppressive king of the Assyrians, who had already gained control of the whole world by the spear and was lifted up against your holy city, speaking grievous words with boasting and insolence, you, O Lord, broke in pieces, showing your power to many nations.

[6] The three companions in Babylon who had voluntarily surrendered their lives to the flames so as not to serve vain things, you rescued unharmed, even to a hair, moistening the fiery furnace with dew and turning the flame against all their enemies.

[7] Daniel, who through envious slanders was cast down into the ground to lions as food for wild beasts, you brought up to the light unharmed.
[8] And Jonah, wasting away in the belly of a huge, sea-born monster, you, Father, watched over and restored unharmed to all his family.
[9] And now, you who hate insolence, all-merciful and protector of all, reveal yourself quickly to those of the nation of Israel -- who are being outrageously treated by the abominable and lawless Gentiles.
[10] Even if our lives have become entangled in impieties in our exile, rescue us from the hand of the enemy, and destroy us, Lord, by whatever fate you choose.
[11] Let not the vain-minded praise their vanities at the destruction of your beloved people, saying, `Not even their god has rescued them.'
[12] But you, O Eternal One, who have all might and all power, watch over us now and have mercy upon us who by the senseless insolence of the lawless are being deprived of life in the manner of traitors.
[13] And let the Gentiles cower today in fear of your invincible might, O honored One, who have power to save the nation of Jacob.
[14] The whole throng of infants and their parents entreat you with tears.
[15] Let it be shown to all the Gentiles that you are with us, O Lord, and have not turned your face from us; but just as you have said, `Not even when they were in the land of their enemies did I neglect them,' so accomplish it, O Lord."
[16] Just as Eleazar was ending his prayer, the king arrived at the hippodrome with the beasts and all the arrogance of his forces.
[17] And when the Jews observed this they raised great cries to heaven so that even the nearby valleys resounded with them and brought an uncontrollable terror upon the army.
[18] Then the most glorious, almighty, and true God revealed his holy face and opened the heavenly gates, from which two glorious angels of fearful aspect descended, visible to all but the Jews.
[19] They opposed the forces of the enemy and filled them with confusion and terror, binding them with immovable shackles.
[20] Even the king began to shudder bodily, and he forgot his sullen insolence.
[21] The beasts turned back upon the armed forces following them and began trampling and destroying them.
[22] Then the king's anger was turned to pity and tears because of the things that he had devised beforehand.
[23] For when he heard the shouting and saw them all fallen headlong to destruction, he wept and angrily threatened his friends, saying,
[24] "You are committing treason and surpassing tyrants in cruelty; and even me, your benefactor, you are now attempting to deprive of dominion and life by secretly devising acts of no advantage to the kingdom.

[25] Who is it that has taken each man from his home and senselessly gathered here those who faithfully have held the fortresses of our country?
[26] Who is it that has so lawlessly encompassed with outrageous treatment those who from the beginning differed from all nations in their goodwill toward us and often have accepted willingly the worst of human dangers?
[27] Loose and untie their unjust bonds! Send them back to their homes in peace, begging pardon for your former actions!
[28] Release the sons of the almighty and living God of heaven, who from the time of our ancestors until now has granted an unimpeded and notable stability to our government."
[29] These then were the things he said; and the Jews, immediately released, praised their holy God and Savior, since they now had escaped death.
[30] Then the king, when he had returned to the city, summoned the official in charge of the revenues and ordered him to provide to the Jews both wines and everything else needed for a festival of seven days, deciding that they should celebrate their rescue with all joyfulness in that same place in which they had expected to meet their destruction.
[31] Accordingly those disgracefully treated and near to death, or rather, who stood at its gates, arranged for a banquet of deliverance instead of a bitter and lamentable death, and full of joy they apportioned to celebrants the place which had been prepared for their destruction and burial.
[32] They ceased their chanting of dirges and took up the song of their fathers, praising God, their Savior and worker of wonders. Putting an end to all mourning and wailing, they formed choruses as a sign of peaceful joy.
[33] Likewise also the king, after convening a great banquet to celebrate these events, gave thanks to heaven unceasingly and lavishly for the unexpected rescue which he had experienced.
[34] And those who had previously believed that the Jews would be destroyed and become food for birds, and had joyfully registered them, groaned as they themselves were overcome by disgrace, and their fire-breathing boldness was ignominiously quenched.
[35] But the Jews, when they had arranged the aforementioned choral group, as we have said before, passed the time in feasting to the accompaniment of joyous thanksgiving and psalms.
[36] And when they had ordained a public rite for these things in their whole community and for their descendants, they instituted the observance of the aforesaid days as a festival, not for drinking and gluttony, but because of the deliverance that had come to them through God.
[37] Then they petitioned the king, asking for dismissal to their homes.

[38] So their registration was carried out from the twenty-fifth of Pachon to the fourth of Epeiph, for forty days; and their destruction was set for the fifth to the seventh of Epeiph, the three days

[39] on which the Lord of all most gloriously revealed his mercy and rescued them all together and unharmed.

[40] Then they feasted, provided with everything by the king, until the fourteenth day, on which also they made the petition for their dismissal.

[41] The king granted their request at once and wrote the following letter for them to the generals in the cities, magnanimously expressing his concern:

3Mac.7

[1] "King Ptolemy Philopator to the generals in Egypt and all in authority in his government, greetings and good health.

[2] We ourselves and our children are faring well, the great God guiding our affairs according to our desire.

[3] Certain of our friends, frequently urging us with malicious intent, persuaded us to gather together the Jews of the kingdom in a body and to punish them with barbarous penalties as traitors;

[4] for they declared that our government would never be firmly established until this was accomplished, because of the ill-will which these people had toward all nations.

[5] They also led them out with harsh treatment as slaves, or rather as traitors, and, girding themselves with a cruelty more savage than that of Scythian custom, they tried without any inquiry or examination to put them to death.

[6] But we very severely threatened them for these acts, and in accordance with the clemency which we have toward all men we barely spared their lives. Since we have come to realize that the God of heaven surely defends the Jews, always taking their part as a father does for his children,

[7] and since we have taken into account the friendly and firm goodwill which they had toward us and our ancestors, we justly have acquitted them of every charge of whatever kind.

[8] We also have ordered each and every one to return to his own home, with no one in any place doing them harm at all or reproaching them for the irrational things that have happened.

[9] For you should know that if we devise any evil against them or cause them any grief at all, we always shall have not man but the Ruler over every power, the Most High God, in everything and inescapably as an antagonist to avenge such acts. Farewell."

[10] Upon receiving this letter the Jews did not immediately hurry to make their departure, but they requested of the king that at their own hands those of the Jewish nation who had willfully transgressed against the holy God and the law of God should receive the punishment they deserved.

[11] For they declared that those who for the belly's sake had transgressed the divine commandments would never be favorably disposed toward the king's government.

[12] The king then, admitting and approving the truth of what they said, granted them a general license so that freely and without royal authority or supervision they might destroy those everywhere in his kingdom who had transgressed the law of God.

[13] When they had applauded him in fitting manner, their priests and the whole multitude shouted the Hallelujah and joyfully departed.

[14] And so on their way they punished and put to a public and shameful death any whom they met of their fellow-countrymen who had become defiled.

[15] In that day they put to death more than three hundred men; and they kept the day as a joyful festival, since they had destroyed the profaners.

[16] But those who had held fast to God even to death and had received the full enjoyment of deliverance began their departure from the city, crowned with all sorts of very fragrant flowers, joyfully and loudly giving thanks to the one God of their fathers, the eternal Savior of Israel, in words of praise and all kinds of melodious songs.

[17] When they had arrived at Ptolemais, called "rose-bearing" because of a characteristic of the place, the fleet waited for them, in accord with the common desire, for seven days.

[18] There they celebrated their deliverance, for the king had generously provided all things to them for their journey, to each as far as his own house.

[19] And when they had landed in peace with appropriate thanksgiving, there too in like manner they decided to observe these days as a joyous festival during the time of their stay.

[20] Then, after inscribing them as holy on a pillar and dedicating a place of prayer at the site of the festival, they departed unharmed, free, and overjoyed, since at the king's command they had been brought safely by land and sea and river each to his own place.

[21] They also possessed greater prestige among their enemies, being held in honor and awe; and they were not subject at all to confiscation of their belongings by any one.

[22] Besides they all recovered all of their property, in accordance with the registration, so that those who held any restored it to them with extreme fear. So the supreme God perfectly performed great deeds for their deliverance.

[23] Blessed be the Deliverer of Israel through all times! Amen.

4 Maccabees

4Mac.1
[1] The subject that I am about to discuss is most philosophical, that is, whether devout reason is sovereign over the emotions. So it is right for me to advise you to pay earnest attention to philosophy.
[2] For the subject is essential to everyone who is seeking knowledge, and in addition it includes the praise of the highest virtue -- I mean, of course, rational judgment.
[3] If, then, it is evident that reason rules over those emotions that hinder self-control, namely, gluttony and lust,
[4] it is also clear that it masters the emotions that hinder one from justice, such as malice, and those that stand in the way of courage, namely anger, fear, and pain.
[5] Some might perhaps ask, "If reason rules the emotions, why is it not sovereign over forgetfulness and ignorance?" Their attempt at argument is ridiculous!
[6] For reason does not rule its own emotions, but those that are opposed to justice, courage, and self-control; and it is not for the purpose of destroying them, but so that one may not give way to them.
[7] I could prove to you from many and various examples that reason is dominant over the emotions,
[8] but I can demonstrate it best from the noble bravery of those who died for the sake of virtue, Eleazar and the seven brothers and their mother.
[9] All of these, by despising sufferings that bring death, demonstrated that reason controls the emotions.
[10] On this anniversary it is fitting for me to praise for their virtues those who, with their mother, died for the sake of nobility and goodness, but I would also call them blessed for the honor in which they are held.
[11] For all people, even their torturers, marveled at their courage and endurance, and they became the cause of the downfall of tyranny over their nation. By their endurance they conquered the tyrant, and thus their native land was purified through them.
[12] I shall shortly have an opportunity to speak of this; but, as my custom is, I shall begin by stating my main principle, and then I shall turn to their story, giving glory to the all-wise God.
[13] Our inquiry, accordingly, is whether reason is sovereign over the emotions.
[14] We shall decide just what reason is and what emotion is, how many kinds of emotions there are, and whether reason rules over all these.
[15] Now reason is the mind that with sound logic prefers the life of wisdom.
[16] Wisdom, next, is the knowledge of divine and human matters and the causes of these.

[17] This, in turn, is education in the law, by which we learn divine matters reverently and human affairs to our advantage.
[18] Now the kinds of wisdom are rational judgment, justice, courage, and self-control.
[19] Rational judgment is supreme over all of these, since by means of it reason rules over the emotions.
[20] The two most comprehensive types of the emotions are pleasure and pain; and each of these is by nature concerned with both body and soul.
[21] The emotions of both pleasure and pain have many consequences.
[22] Thus desire precedes pleasure and delight follows it.
[23] Fear precedes pain and sorrow comes after.
[24] Anger, as a man will see if he reflects on this experience, is an emotion embracing pleasure and pain.
[25] In pleasure there exists even a malevolent tendency, which is the most complex of all the emotions.
[26] In the soul it is boastfulness, covetousness, thirst for honor, rivalry, and malice;
[27] in the body, indiscriminate eating, gluttony, and solitary gormandizing.
[28] Just as pleasure and pain are two plants growing from the body and the soul, so there are many offshoots of these plants,
[29] each of which the master cultivator, reason, weeds and prunes and ties up and waters and thoroughly irrigates, and so tames the jungle of habits and emotions.
[30] For reason is the guide of the virtues, but over the emotions it is sovereign. Observe now first of all that rational judgment is sovereign over the emotions by virtue of the restraining power of self-control.
[31] Self-control, then, is dominance over the desires.
[32] Some desires are mental, others are physical, and reason obviously rules over both.
[33] Otherwise how is it that when we are attracted to forbidden foods we abstain from the pleasure to be had from them? Is it not because reason is able to rule over appetites? I for one think so.
[34] Therefore when we crave seafood and fowl and animals and all sorts of foods that are forbidden to us by the law, we abstain because of domination by reason.
[35] For the emotions of the appetites are restrained, checked by the temperate mind, and all the impulses of the body are bridled by reason.
4Mac.2
[1] And why is it amazing that the desires of the mind for the enjoyment of beauty are rendered powerless?
[2] It is for this reason, certainly, that the temperate Joseph is praised, because by mental effort he overcame sexual desire.

[3] For when he was young and in his prime for intercourse, by his reason he nullified the frenzy of the passions.
[4] Not only is reason proved to rule over the frenzied urge of sexual desire, but also over every desire.
[5] Thus the law says, "You shall not covet your neighbor's wife...or anything that is your neighbor's."
[6] In fact, since the law has told us not to covet, I could prove to you all the more that reason is able to control desires. Just so it is with the emotions that hinder one from justice.
[7] Otherwise how could it be that someone who is habitually a solitary gormandizer, a glutton, or even a drunkard can learn a better way, unless reason is clearly lord of the emotions?
[8] Thus, as soon as a man adopts a way of life in accordance with the law, even though he is a lover of money, he is forced to act contrary to his natural ways and to lend without interest to the needy and to cancel the debt when the seventh year arrives.
[9] If one is greedy, he is ruled by the law through his reason so that he neither gleans his harvest nor gathers the last grapes from the vineyard. In all other matters we can recognize that reason rules the emotions.
[10] For the law prevails even over affection for parents, so that virtue is not abandoned for their sakes.
[11] It is superior to love for one's wife, so that one rebukes her when she breaks the law.
[12] It takes precedence over love for children, so that one punishes them for misdeeds.
[13] It is sovereign over the relationship of friends, so that one rebukes friends when they act wickedly.
[14] Do not consider it paradoxical when reason, through the law, can prevail even over enmity. The fruit trees of the enemy are not cut down, but one preserves the property of enemies from the destroyers and helps raise up what has fallen.
[15] It is evident that reason rules even the more violent emotions: lust for power, vainglory, boasting, arrogance, and malice.
[16] For the temperate mind repels all these malicious emotions, just as it repels anger -- for it is sovereign over even this.
[17] When Moses was angry with Dathan and Abiram he did nothing against them in anger, but controlled his anger by reason.
[18] For, as I have said, the temperate mind is able to get the better of the emotions, to correct some, and to render others powerless.
[19] Why else did Jacob, our most wise father, censure the households of Simeon and Levi for their irrational slaughter of the entire tribe of the Shechemites, saying, "Cursed be their anger"?
[20] For if reason could not control anger, he would not have spoken thus.

[21] Now when God fashioned man, he planted in him emotions and inclinations,

[22] but at the same time he enthroned the mind among the senses as a sacred governor over them all.

[23] To the mind he gave the law; and one who lives subject to this will rule a kingdom that is temperate, just, good, and courageous.

[24] How is it then, one might say, that if reason is master of the emotions, it does not control forgetfulness and ignorance?

4Mac.3

[1] This notion is entirely ridiculous; for it is evident that reason rules not over its own emotions, but over those of the body.

[2] No one of us can eradicate that kind of desire, but reason can provide a way for us not to be enslaved by desire.

[3] No one of us can eradicate anger from the mind, but reason can help to deal with anger.

[4] No one of us can eradicate malice, but reason can fight at our side so that we are not overcome by malice.

[5] For reason does not uproot the emotions but is their antagonist.

[6] Now this can be explained more clearly by the story of King David's thirst.

[7] David had been attacking the Philistines all day long, and together with the soldiers of his nation had slain many of them.

[8] Then when evening fell, he came, sweating and quite exhausted, to the royal tent, around which the whole army of our ancestors had encamped.

[9] Now all the rest were at supper,

[10] but the king was extremely thirsty, and although springs were plentiful there, he could not satisfy his thirst from them.

[11] But a certain irrational desire for the water in the enemy's territory tormented and inflamed him, undid and consumed him.

[12] When his guards complained bitterly because of the king's craving, two staunch young soldiers, respecting the king's desire, armed themselves fully, and taking a pitcher climbed over the enemy's ramparts.

[13] Eluding the sentinels at the gates, they went searching throughout the enemy camp

[14] and found the spring, and from it boldly brought the king a drink.

[15] But David, although he was burning with thirst, considered it an altogether fearful danger to his soul to drink what was regarded as equivalent to blood.

[16] Therefore, opposing reason to desire, he poured out the drink as an offering to God.

[17] For the temperate mind can conquer the drives of the emotions and quench the flames of frenzied desires;

[18] it can overthrow bodily agonies even when they are extreme, and by nobility of reason spurn all domination by the emotions.

[19] The present occasion now invites us to a narrative demonstration of temperate reason.

[20] At a time when our fathers were enjoying profound peace because of their observance of the law and were prospering, so that even Seleucus Nicanor, king of Asia, had both appropriated money to them for the temple service and recognized their commonwealth --

[21] just at that time certain men attempted a revolution against the public harmony and caused many and various disasters.

4Mac.4

[1] Now there was a certain Simon, a political opponent of the noble and good man, Onias, who then held the high priesthood for life. When despite all manner of slander he was unable to injure Onias in the eyes of the nation, he fled the country with the purpose of betraying it.

[2] So he came to Apollonius, governor of Syria, Phoenicia, and Cilicia, and said,

[3] "I have come here because I am loyal to the king's government, to report that in the Jerusalem treasuries there are deposited tens of thousands in private funds, which are not the property of the temple but belong to King Seleucus."

[4] When Apollonius learned the details of these things, he praised Simon for his service to the king and went up to Seleucus to inform him of the rich treasure.

[5] On receiving authority to deal with this matter, he proceeded quickly to our country accompanied by the accursed Simon and a very strong military force.

[6] He said that he had come with the king's authority to seize the private funds in the treasury.

[7] The people indignantly protested his words, considering it outrageous that those who had committed deposits to the sacred treasury should be deprived of them, and did all that they could to prevent it.

[8] But, uttering threats, Apollonius went on to the temple.

[9] While the priests together with women and children were imploring God in the temple to shield the holy place that was being treated so contemptuously,

[10] and while Apollonius was going up with his armed forces to seize the money, angels on horseback with lightning flashing from their weapons appeared from heaven, instilling in them great fear and trembling.

[11] Then Apollonius fell down half dead in the temple area that was open to all, stretched out his hands toward heaven, and with tears besought the Hebrews to pray for him and propitiate the wrath of the heavenly army.

[12] For he said that he had committed a sin deserving of death, and that if he were delivered he would praise the blessedness of the holy place before all people.

[13] Moved by these words, Onias the high priest, although otherwise he had scruples about doing so, prayed for him lest King Seleucus suppose that Apollonius had been overcome by human treachery and not by divine justice.

[14] So Apollonius, having been preserved beyond all expectations, went away to report to the king what had happened to him.

[15] When King Seleucus died, his son Antiochus Epiphanes succeeded to the throne, an arrogant and terrible man,

[16] who removed Onias from the priesthood and appointed Onias's brother Jason as high priest.

[17] Jason agreed that if the office were conferred upon him he would pay the king three thousand six hundred and sixty talents annually.

[18] So the king appointed him high priest and ruler of the nation.

[19] Jason changed the nation's way of life and altered its form of government in complete violation of the law,

[20] so that not only was a gymnasium constructed at the very citadel of our native land, but also the temple service was abolished.

[21] The divine justice was angered by these acts and caused Antiochus himself to make war on them.

[22] For when he was warring against Ptolemy in Egypt, he heard that a rumor of his death had spread and that the people of Jerusalem had rejoiced greatly. He speedily marched against them,

[23] and after he had plundered them he issued a decree that if any of them should be found observing the ancestral law they should die.

[24] When, by means of his decrees, he had not been able in any way to put an end to the people's observance of the law, but saw that all his threats and punishments were being disregarded,

[25] even to the point that women, because they had circumcised their sons, were thrown headlong from heights along with their infants, though they had known beforehand that they would suffer this --

[26] when, then, his decrees were despised by the people, he himself, through torture, tried to compel everyone in the nation to eat defiling foods and to renounce Judaism.

4Mac.5

[1] The tyrant Antiochus, sitting in state with his counselors on a certain high place, and with his armed soldiers standing about him,

[2] ordered the guards to seize each and every Hebrew and to compel them to eat pork and food sacrificed to idols.

[3] If any were not willing to eat defiling food, they were to be broken on the wheel and killed.

[4] And when many persons had been rounded up, one man, Eleazar by name, leader of the flock, was brought before the king. He was a man of priestly family, learned in the law, advanced in age, and known to many in the tyrant's court because of his philosophy.

Joseph Lumpkin

[5] When Antiochus saw him he said,
[6] "Before I begin to torture you, old man, I would advise you to save yourself by eating pork,
[7] for I respect your age and your gray hairs. Although you have had them for so long a time, it does not seem to me that you are a philosopher when you observe the religion of the Jews.
[8] Why, when nature has granted it to us, should you abhor eating the very excellent meat of this animal?
[9] It is senseless not to enjoy delicious things that are not shameful, and wrong to spurn the gifts of nature.
[10] It seems to me that you will do something even more senseless if, by holding a vain opinion concerning the truth, you continue to despise me to your own hurt.
[11] Will you not awaken from your foolish philosophy, dispel your futile reasonings, adopt a mind appropriate to your years, philosophize according to the truth of what is beneficial,
[12] and have compassion on your old age by honoring my humane advice?
[13] For consider this, that if there is some power watching over this religion of yours, it will excuse you from any transgression that arises out of compulsion."
[14] When the tyrant urged him in this fashion to eat meat unlawfully, Eleazar asked to have a word.
[15] When he had received permission to speak, he began to address the people as follows:
[16] "We, O Antiochus, who have been persuaded to govern our lives by the divine law, think that there is no compulsion more powerful than our obedience to the law.
[17] Therefore we consider that we should not transgress it in any respect.
[18] Even if, as you suppose, our law were not truly divine and we had wrongly held it to be divine, not even so would it be right for us to invalidate our reputation for piety.
[19] Therefore do not suppose that it would be a petty sin if we were to eat defiling food;
[20] to transgress the law in matters either small or great is of equal seriousness,
[21] for in either case the law is equally despised.
[22] You scoff at our philosophy as though living by it were irrational,
[23] but it teaches us self-control, so that we master all pleasures and desires, and it also trains us in courage, so that we endure any suffering willingly;
[24] it instructs us in justice, so that in all our dealings we act impartially, and it teaches us piety, so that with proper reverence we worship the only real God.

[25] "Therefore we do not eat defiling food; for since we believe that the law was established by God, we know that in the nature of things the Creator of the world in giving us the law has shown sympathy toward us.
[26] He has permitted us to eat what will be most suitable for our lives, but he has forbidden us to eat meats that would be contrary to this.
[27] It would be tyrannical for you to compel us not only to transgress the law, but also to eat in such a way that you may deride us for eating defiling foods, which are most hateful to us.
[28] But you shall have no such occasion to laugh at me,
[29] nor will I transgress the sacred oaths of my ancestors concerning the keeping of the law,
[30] not even if you gouge out my eyes and burn my entrails.
[31] I am not so old and cowardly as not to be young in reason on behalf of piety.
[32] Therefore get your torture wheels ready and fan the fire more vehemently!
[33] I do not so pity my old age as to break the ancestral law by my own act.
[34] I will not play false to you, O law that trained me, nor will I renounce you, beloved self-control.
[35] I will not put you to shame, philosophical reason, nor will I reject you, honored priesthood and knowledge of the law.
[36] You, O king, shall not stain the honorable mouth of my old age, nor my long life lived lawfully.
[37] The fathers will receive me as pure, as one who does not fear your violence even to death.
[38] You may tyrannize the ungodly, but you shall not dominate my religious principles either by word or by deed."
4Mac.6
[1] When Eleazar in this manner had made eloquent response to the exhortations of the tyrant, the guards who were standing by dragged him violently to the instruments of torture.
[2] First they stripped the old man, who remained adorned with the gracefulness of his piety.
[3] And after they had tied his arms on each side they scourged him,
[4] while a herald opposite him cried out, "Obey the king's commands!"
[5] But the courageous and noble man, as a true Eleazar, was unmoved, as though being tortured in a dream;
[6] yet while the old man's eyes were raised to heaven, his flesh was being torn by scourges, his blood flowing, and his sides were being cut to pieces.
[7] And though he fell to the ground because his body could not endure the agonies, he kept his reason upright and unswerving.
[8] One of the cruel guards rushed at him and began to kick him in the side to make him get up again after he fell.

[9] But he bore the pains and scorned the punishment and endured the tortures.

[10] And like a noble athlete the old man, while being beaten, was victorious over his torturers;

[11] in fact, with his face bathed in sweat, and gasping heavily for breath, he amazed even his torturers by his courageous spirit.

[12] At that point, partly out of pity for his old age,

[13] partly out of sympathy from their acquaintance with him, partly out of admiration for his endurance, some of the king's retinue came to him and said,

[14] "Eleazar, why are you so irrationally destroying yourself through these evil things?

[15] We will set before you some cooked meat; save yourself by pretending to eat pork."

[16] But Eleazar, as though more bitterly tormented by this counsel, cried out:

[17] "May we, the children of Abraham, never think so basely that out of cowardice we feign a role unbecoming to us!

[18] For it would be irrational if we, who have lived in accordance with truth to old age and have maintained in accordance with law the reputation of such a life, should now change our course

[19] become a pattern of impiety to the young, in becoming an example of the eating of defiling food.

[20] It would be shameful if we should survive for a little while and during that time be a laughing stock to all for our cowardice,

[21] and if we should be despised by the tyrant as unmanly, and not protect our divine law even to death.

[22] Therefore, O children of Abraham, die nobly for your religion!

[23] And you, guards of the tyrant, why do you delay?"

[24] When they saw that he was so courageous in the face of the afflictions, and that he had not been changed by their compassion, the guards brought him to the fire.

[25] There they burned him with maliciously contrived instruments, threw him down, and poured stinking liquids into his nostrils.

[26] When he was now burned to his very bones and about to expire, he lifted up his eyes to God and said,

[27] "You know, O God, that though I might have saved myself, I am dying in burning torments for the sake of the law.

[28] Be merciful to your people, and let our punishment suffice for them.

[29] Make my blood their purification, and take my life in exchange for theirs."

[30] And after he said this, the holy man died nobly in his tortures, and by reason he resisted even to the very tortures of death for the sake of the law.

[31] Admittedly, then, devout reason is sovereign over the emotions.

[32] For if the emotions had prevailed over reason, we would have testified to their domination.

[33] But now that reason has conquered the emotions, we properly attribute to it the power to govern.

[34] And it is right for us to acknowledge the dominance of reason when it masters even external agonies. It would be ridiculous to deny it.

[35] And I have proved not only that reason has mastered agonies, but also that it masters pleasures and in no respect yields to them.

4Mac.7

[1] For like a most skilful pilot, the reason of our father Eleazar steered the ship of religion over the sea of the emotions,

[2] and though buffeted by the stormings of the tyrant and overwhelmed by the mighty waves of tortures,

[3] in no way did he turn the rudder of religion until he sailed into the haven of immortal victory.

[4] No city besieged with many ingenious war machines has ever held out as did that most holy man. Although his sacred life was consumed by tortures and racks, he conquered the besiegers with the shield of his devout reason.

[5] For in setting his mind firm like a jutting cliff, our father Eleazar broke the maddening waves of the emotions.

[6] O priest, worthy of the priesthood, you neither defiled your sacred teeth nor profaned your stomach, which had room only for reverence and purity, by eating defiling foods.

[7] O man in harmony with the law and philosopher of divine life!

[8] Such should be those who are administrators of the law, shielding it with their own blood and noble sweat in sufferings even to death.

[9] You, father, strengthened our loyalty to the law through your glorious endurance, and you did not abandon the holiness which you praised, but by your deeds you made your words of divine philosophy credible.

[10] O aged man, more powerful than tortures; O elder, fiercer than fire; O supreme king over the passions, Eleazar!

[11] For just as our father Aaron, armed with the censer, ran through the multitude of the people and conquered the fiery angel,

[12] so the descendant of Aaron, Eleazar, though being consumed by the fire, remained unmoved in his reason.

[13] Most amazing, indeed, though he was an old man, his body no longer tense and firm, his muscles flabby, his sinews feeble, he became young again

[14] in spirit through reason; and by reason like that of Isaac he rendered the many-headed rack ineffective.

[15] O man of blessed age and of venerable gray hair and of law-abiding life, whom the faithful seal of death has perfected!

[16] If, therefore, because of piety an aged man despised tortures even to death, most certainly devout reason is governor of the emotions.
[17] Some perhaps might say, "Not every one has full command of his emotions, because not every one has prudent reason."
[18] But as many as attend to religion with a whole heart, these alone are able to control the passions of the flesh,
[19] since they believe that they, like our patriarchs Abraham and Isaac and Jacob, do not die to God, but live in God.
[20] No contradiction therefore arises when some persons appear to be dominated by their emotions because of the weakness of their reason.
[21] What person who lives as a philosopher by the whole rule of philosophy, and trusts in God,
[22] and knows that it is blessed to endure any suffering for the sake of virtue, would not be able to overcome the emotions through godliness?
[23] For only the wise and courageous man is lord of his emotions.
4Mac.8
[1] For this is why even the very young, by following a philosophy in accordance with devout reason, have prevailed over the most painful instruments of torture.
[2] For when the tyrant was conspicuously defeated in his first attempt, being unable to compel an aged man to eat defiling foods, then in violent rage he commanded that others of the Hebrew captives be brought, and that any who ate defiling food should be freed after eating, but if any were to refuse, these should be tortured even more cruelly.
[3] When the tyrant had given these orders, seven brothers -- handsome, modest, noble, and accomplished in every way -- were brought before him along with their aged mother.
[4] When the tyrant saw them, grouped about their mother as if in a chorus, he was pleased with them. And struck by their appearance and nobility, he smiled at them, and summoned them nearer and said,
[5] "Young men, I admire each and every one of you in a kindly manner, and greatly respect the beauty and the number of such brothers. Not only do I advise you not to display the same madness as that of the old man who has just been tortured, but I also exhort you to yield to me and enjoy my friendship.
[6] Just as I am able to punish those who disobey my orders, so I can be a benefactor to those who obey me.
[7] Trust me, then, and you will have positions of authority in my government if you will renounce the ancestral tradition of your national life.
[8] And enjoy your youth by adopting the Greek way of life and by changing your manner of living.

[9] But if by disobedience you rouse my anger, you will compel me to destroy each and every one of you with dreadful punishments through tortures.

[10] Therefore take pity on yourselves. Even I, your enemy, have compassion for your youth and handsome appearance.

[11] Will you not consider this, that if you disobey, nothing remains for you but to die on the rack?"

[12] When he had said these things, he ordered the instruments of torture to be brought forward so as to persuade them out of fear to eat the defiling food.

[13] And when the guards had placed before them wheels and joint-dislocators, rack and hooks and catapults and caldrons, braziers and thumbscrews and iron claws and wedges and bellows, the tyrant resumed speaking:

[14] "Be afraid, young fellows, and whatever justice you revere will be merciful to you when you transgress under compulsion."

[15] But when they had heard the inducements and saw the dreadful devices, not only were they not afraid, but they also opposed the tyrant with their own philosophy, and by their right reasoning nullified his tyranny.

[16] Let us consider, on the other hand, what arguments might have been used if some of them had been cowardly and unmanly. Would they not have been these?

[17] "O wretches that we are and so senseless! Since the king has summoned and exhorted us to accept kind treatment if we obey him,

[18] why do we take pleasure in vain resolves and venture upon a disobedience that brings death?

[19] O men and brothers, should we not fear the instruments of torture and consider the threats of torments, and give up this vain opinion and this arrogance that threatens to destroy us?

[20] Let us take pity on our youth and have compassion on our mother's age;

[21] and let us seriously consider that if we disobey we are dead!

[22] Also, divine justice will excuse us for fearing the king when we are under compulsion.

[23] Why do we banish ourselves from this most pleasant life and deprive ourselves of this delightful world?

[24] Let us not struggle against compulsion nor take hollow pride in being put to the rack.

[25] Not even the law itself would arbitrarily slay us for fearing the instruments of torture.

[26] Why does such contentiousness excite us and such a fatal stubbornness please us, when we can live in peace if we obey the king?"

[27] But the youths, though about to be tortured, neither said any of these things nor even seriously considered them.

[28] For they were contemptuous of the emotions and sovereign over agonies,

[29] so that as soon as the tyrant had ceased counseling them to eat defiling food, all with one voice together, as from one mind, said:

4Mac.9

[1] "Why do you delay, O tyrant? For we are ready to die rather than transgress our ancestral commandments;

[2] we are obviously putting our forefathers to shame unless we should practice ready obedience to the law and to Moses our counselor.

[3] Tyrant and counselor of lawlessness, in your hatred for us do not pity us more than we pity ourselves.

[4] For we consider this pity of yours which insures our safety through transgression of the law to be more grievous than death itself.

[5] You are trying to terrify us by threatening us with death by torture, as though a short time ago you learned nothing from Eleazar.

[6] And if the aged men of the Hebrews because of their religion lived piously while enduring torture, it would be even more fitting that we young men should die despising your coercive tortures, which our aged instructor also overcame.

[7] Therefore, tyrant, put us to the test; and if you take our lives because of our religion, do not suppose that you can injure us by torturing us.

[8] For we, through this severe suffering and endurance, shall have the prize of virtue and shall be with God, for whom we suffer;

[9] but you, because of your bloodthirstiness toward us, will deservedly undergo from the divine justice eternal torment by fire."

[10] When they had said these things the tyrant not only was angry, as at those who are disobedient, but also was enraged, as at those who are ungrateful.

[11] Then at his command the guards brought forward the eldest, and having torn off his tunic, they bound his hands and arms with thongs on each side.

[12] When they had worn themselves out beating him with scourges, without accomplishing anything, they placed him upon the wheel.

[13] When the noble youth was stretched out around this, his limbs were dislocated,

[14] and though broken in every member he denounced the tyrant, saying,

[15] "Most abominable tyrant, enemy of heavenly justice, savage of mind, you are mangling me in this manner, not because I am a murderer, or as one who acts impiously, but because I protect the divine law."

[16] And when the guards said, "Agree to eat so that you may be released from the tortures,"

[17] he replied, "You abominable lackeys, your wheel is not so powerful as to strangle my reason. Cut my limbs, burn my flesh, and twist my joints.
[18] Through all these tortures I will convince you that sons of the Hebrews alone are invincible where virtue is concerned."
[19] While he was saying these things, they spread fire under him, and while fanning the flames they tightened the wheel further.
[20] The wheel was completely smeared with blood, and the heap of coals was being quenched by the drippings of gore, and pieces of flesh were falling off the axles of the machine.
[21] Although the ligaments joining his bones were already severed, the courageous youth, worthy of Abraham, did not groan,
[22] but as though transformed by fire into immortality he nobly endured the rackings.
[23] "Imitate me, brothers," he said. "Do not leave your post in my struggle or renounce our courageous brotherhood.
[24] Fight the sacred and noble battle for religion. Thereby the just Providence of our ancestors may become merciful to our nation and take vengeance on the accursed tyrant."
[25] When he had said this, the saintly youth broke the thread of life.
[26] While all were marveling at his courageous spirit, the guards brought in the next eldest, and after fitting themselves with iron gauntlets having sharp hooks, they bound him to the torture machine and catapult.
[27] Before torturing him, they inquired if he were willing to eat, and they heard this noble decision.
[28] These leopard-like beasts tore out his sinews with the iron hands, flayed all his flesh up to his chin, and tore away his scalp. But he steadfastly endured this agony and said,
[29] "How sweet is any kind of death for the religion of our fathers!"
[30] To the tyrant he said, "Do you not think, you most savage tyrant, that you are being tortured more than I, as you see the arrogant design of your tyranny being defeated by our endurance for the sake of religion?
[31] I lighten my pain by the joys that come from virtue,
[32] but you suffer torture by the threats that come from impiety. You will not escape, most abominable tyrant, the judgments of the divine wrath."
4Mac.10
[1] When he too had endured a glorious death, the third was led in, and many repeatedly urged him to save himself by tasting the meat.
[2] But he shouted, "Do you not know that the same father begot me and those who died, and the same mother bore me, and that I was brought up on the same teachings?
[3] I do not renounce the noble kinship that binds me to my brothers."
[4]

[5] Enraged by the man's boldness, they disjointed his hands and feet with their instruments, dismembering him by prying his limbs from their sockets,

[6] and breaking his fingers and arms and legs and elbows.

[7] Since they were not able in any way to break his spirit, they abandoned the instruments and scalped him with their fingernails in a Scythian fashion.

[8] They immediately brought him to the wheel, and while his vertebrae were being dislocated upon it he saw his own flesh torn all around and drops of blood flowing from his entrails.

[9] When he was about to die, he said,

[10] "We, most abominable tyrant, are suffering because of our godly training and virtue,

[11] but you, because of your impiety and bloodthirstiness, will undergo unceasing torments."

[12] When he also had died in a manner worthy of his brothers, they dragged in the fourth, saying,

[13] "As for you, do not give way to the same insanity as your brothers, but obey the king and save yourself."

[14] But he said to them, "You do not have a fire hot enough to make me play the coward.

[15] No, by the blessed death of my brothers, by the eternal destruction of the tyrant, and by the everlasting life of the pious, I will not renounce our noble brotherhood.

[16] Contrive tortures, tyrant, so that you may learn from them that I am a brother to those who have just been tortured."

[17] When he heard this, the bloodthirsty, murderous, and utterly abominable Antiochus gave orders to cut out his tongue.

[18] But he said, "Even if you remove my organ of speech, God hears also those who are mute.

[19] See, here is my tongue; cut it off, for in spite of this you will not make our reason speechless.

[20] Gladly, for the sake of God, we let our bodily members be mutilated.

[21] God will visit you swiftly, for you are cutting out a tongue that has been melodious with divine hymns."

4Mac.11

[1] When this one died also, after being cruelly tortured, the fifth leaped up, saying,

[2] "I will not refuse, tyrant, to be tortured for the sake of virtue.

[3] I have come of my own accord, so that by murdering me you will incur punishment from the heavenly justice for even more crimes.

[4] Hater of virtue, hater of mankind, for what act of ours are you destroying us in this way?

[5] Is it because we revere the Creator of all things and live according to his virtuous law?

[6] But these deeds deserve honors, not tortures."

[7]

[9] While he was saying these things, the guards bound him and dragged him to the catapult;

[10] they tied him to it on his knees, and fitting iron clamps on them, they twisted his back around the wedge on the wheel, so that he was completely curled back like a scorpion, and all his members were disjointed.

[11] In this condition, gasping for breath and in anguish of body,

[12] he said, "Tyrant, they are splendid favors that you grant us against your will, because through these noble sufferings you give us an opportunity to show our endurance for the law."

[13] After he too had died, the sixth, a mere boy, was led in. When the tyrant inquired whether he was willing to eat and be released, he said,

[14] "I am younger in age than my brothers, but I am their equal in mind.

[15] Since to this end we were born and bred, we ought likewise to die for the same principles.

[16] So if you intend to torture me for not eating defiling foods, go on torturing!"

[17] When he had said this, they led him to the wheel.

[18] He was carefully stretched tight upon it, his back was broken, and he was roasted from underneath.

[19] To his back they applied sharp spits that had been heated in the fire, and pierced his ribs so that his entrails were burned through.

[20] While being tortured he said, "O contest befitting holiness, in which so many of us brothers have been summoned to an arena of sufferings for religion, and in which we have not been defeated!

[21] For religious knowledge, O tyrant, is invincible.

[22] I also, equipped with nobility, will die with my brothers,

[23] and I myself will bring a great avenger upon you, you inventor of tortures and enemy of those who are truly devout.

[24] We six boys have paralyzed your tyranny!

[25] Since you have not been able to persuade us to change our mind or to force us to eat defiling foods, is not this your downfall?

[26] Your fire is cold to us, and the catapults painless, and your violence powerless.

[27] For it is not the guards of the tyrant but those of the divine law that are set over us; therefore, unconquered, we hold fast to reason."

4Mac.12

[1] When he also, thrown into the caldron, had died a blessed death, the seventh and youngest of all came forward.

[2] Even though the tyrant had been fearfully reproached by the brothers, he felt strong compassion for this child when he saw that he was already in fetters. He summoned him to come nearer and tried to console him, saying,

[3] "You see the result of your brothers' stupidity, for they died in torments because of their disobedience.

[4] You too, if you do not obey, will be miserably tortured and die before your time,

[5] but if you yield to persuasion you will be my friend and a leader in the government of the kingdom."

[6] When he had so pleaded, he sent for the boy's mother to show compassion on her who had been bereaved of so many sons and to influence her to persuade the surviving son to obey and save himself.

[7] But when his mother had exhorted him in the Hebrew language, as we shall tell a little later,

[8] he said, "Let me loose, let me speak to the king and to all his friends that are with him."

[9] Extremely pleased by the boy's declaration, they freed him at once.

[10] Running to the nearest of the braziers,

[11] he said, "You profane tyrant, most impious of all the wicked, since you have received good things and also your kingdom from God, were you not ashamed to murder his servants and torture on the wheel those who practice religion?

[12] Because of this, justice has laid up for you intense and eternal fire and tortures, and these throughout all time will never let you go.

[13] As a man, were you not ashamed, you most savage beast, to cut out the tongues of men who have feelings like yours and are made of the same elements as you, and to maltreat and torture them in this way?

[14] Surely they by dying nobly fulfilled their service to God, but you will wail bitterly for having slain without cause the contestants for virtue."

[15] Then because he too was about to die, he said,

[16] "I do not desert the excellent example of my brothers,

[17] and I call on the God of our fathers to be merciful to our nation;

[18] but on you he will take vengeance both in this present life and when you are dead."

[19] After he had uttered these imprecations, he flung himself into the braziers and so ended his life.

4Mac.13

[1] Since, then, the seven brothers despised sufferings even unto death, everyone must concede that devout reason is sovereign over the emotions.

[2] For if they had been slaves to their emotions and had eaten defiling food, we would say that they had been conquered by these emotions.

[3] But in fact it was not so. Instead, by reason, which is praised before God, they prevailed over their emotions.

[4] The supremacy of the mind over these cannot be overlooked, for the brothers mastered both emotions and pains.

[5] How then can one fail to confess the sovereignty of right reason over emotion in those who were not turned back by fiery agonies?

[6] For just as towers jutting out over harbors hold back the threatening waves and make it calm for those who sail into the inner basin,

[7] so the seven-towered right reason of the youths, by fortifying the harbor of religion, conquered the tempest of the emotions.

[8] For they constituted a holy chorus of religion and encouraged one another, saying,

[9] "Brothers, let us die like brothers for the sake of the law; let us imitate the three youths in Assyria who despised the same ordeal of the furnace.

[10] Let us not be cowardly in the demonstration of our piety."

[11] While one said, "Courage, brother," another said, "Bear up nobly,"

[12] and another reminded them, "Remember whence you came, and the father by whose hand Isaac would have submitted to being slain for the sake of religion."

[13] Each of them and all of them together looking at one another, cheerful and undaunted, said, "Let us with all our hearts consecrate ourselves to God, who gave us our lives, and let us use our bodies as a bulwark for the law.

[14] Let us not fear him who thinks he is killing us,

[15] for great is the struggle of the soul and the danger of eternal torment lying before those who transgress the commandment of God.

[16] Therefore let us put on the full armor of self-control, which is divine reason.

[17] For if we so die, Abraham and Isaac and Jacob will welcome us, and all the fathers will praise us."

[18] Those who were left behind said to each of the brothers who were being dragged away, "Do not put us to shame, brother, or betray the brothers who have died before us."

[19] You are not ignorant of the affection of brotherhood, which the divine and all-wise Providence has bequeathed through the fathers to their descendants and which was implanted in the mother's womb.

[20] There each of the brothers dwelt the same length of time and was shaped during the same period of time; and growing from the same blood and through the same life, they were brought to the light of day.

[21] When they were born after an equal time of gestation, they drank milk from the same fountains. For such embraces brotherly-loving souls are nourished;

[22] and they grow stronger from this common nurture and daily companionship, and from both general education and our discipline in the law of God.

[23] Therefore, when sympathy and brotherly affection had been so established, the brothers were the more sympathetic to one another.
[24] Since they had been educated by the same law and trained in the same virtues and brought up in right living, they loved one another all the more.
[25] A common zeal for nobility expanded their goodwill and harmony toward one another,
[26] because, with the aid of their religion, they rendered their brotherly love more fervent.
[27] But although nature and companionship and virtuous habits had augmented the affection of brotherhood, those who were left endured for the sake of religion, while watching their brothers being maltreated and tortured to death.
4Mac.14
[1] Furthermore, they encouraged them to face the torture, so that they not only despised their agonies, but also mastered the emotions of brotherly love.
[2] O reason, more royal than kings and freer than the free!
[3] O sacred and harmonious concord of the seven brothers on behalf of religion!
[4] None of the seven youths proved coward or shrank from death,
[5] but all of them, as though running the course toward immortality, hastened to death by torture.
[6] Just as the hands and feet are moved in harmony with the guidance of the mind, so those holy youths, as though moved by an immortal spirit of devotion, agreed to go to death for its sake.
[7] O most holy seven, brothers in harmony! For just as the seven days of creation move in choral dance around religion,
[8] so these youths, forming a chorus, encircled the sevenfold fear of tortures and dissolved it.
[9] Even now, we ourselves shudder as we hear of the tribulations of these young men; they not only saw what was happening, yes, not only heard the direct word of threat, but also bore the sufferings patiently, and in agonies of fire at that.
[10] What could be more excruciatingly painful than this? For the power of fire is intense and swift, and it consumed their bodies quickly.
[11] Do not consider it amazing that reason had full command over these men in their tortures, since the mind of woman despised even more diverse agonies,
[12] for the mother of the seven young men bore up under the rackings of each one of her children.
[13] Observe how complex is a mother's love for her children, which draws everything toward an emotion felt in her inmost parts.
[14] Even unreasoning animals, like mankind, have a sympathy and parental love for their offspring.

[15] For example, among birds, the ones that are tame protect their young by building on the housetops,

[16] and the others, by building in precipitous chasms and in holes and tops of trees, hatch the nestlings and ward off the intruder.

[17] If they are not able to keep him away, they do what they can to help their young by flying in circles around them in the anguish of love, warning them with their own calls.

[18] And why is it necessary to demonstrate sympathy for children by the example of unreasoning animals,

[19] since even bees at the time for making honeycombs defend themselves against intruders as though with an iron dart sting those who approach their hive and defend it even to the death?

[20] But sympathy for her children did not sway the mother of the young men; she was of the same mind as Abraham.

4Mac.15

[1] O reason of the children, tyrant over the emotions! O religion, more desirable to the mother than her children!

[2] Two courses were open to this mother, that of religion, and that of preserving her seven sons for a time, as the tyrant had promised.

[3] She loved religion more, religion that preserves them for eternal life according to God's promise.

[4] In what manner might I express the emotions of parents who love their children? We impress upon the character of a small child a wondrous likeness both of mind and of form. Especially is this true of mothers, who because of their birthpangs have a deeper sympathy toward their offspring than do the fathers.

[5] Considering that mothers are the weaker sex and give birth to many, they are more devoted to their children.

[6] The mother of the seven boys, more than any other mother, loved her children. In seven pregnancies she had implanted in herself tender love toward them,

[7] and because of the many pains she suffered with each of them she had sympathy for them;

[8] yet because of the fear of God she disdained the temporary safety of her children.

[9] Not only so, but also because of the nobility of her sons and their ready obedience to the law she felt a greater tenderness toward them.

[10] For they were righteous and self-controlled and brave and magnanimous, and loved their brothers and their mother, so that they obeyed her even to death in keeping the ordinances.

[11] Nevertheless, though so many factors influenced the mother to suffer with them out of love for her children, in the case of none of them were the various tortures strong enough to pervert her reason.

[12] Instead, the mother urged them on, each child singly and all together, to death for the sake of religion.

[13] O sacred nature and affection of parental love, yearning of parents toward offspring, nurture and indomitable suffering by mothers!

[14] This mother, who saw them tortured and burned one by one, because of religion did not change her attitude.

[15] She watched the flesh of her children consumed by fire, their toes and fingers scattered on the ground, and the flesh of the head to the chin exposed like masks.

[16] O mother, tried now by more bitter pains than even the birth-pangs you suffered for them!

[17] O woman, who alone gave birth to such complete devotion!

[18] When the first-born breathed his last it did not turn you aside, nor when the second in torments looked at you piteously nor when the third expired;

[19] nor did you weep when you looked at the eyes of each one in his tortures gazing boldly at the same agonies, and saw in their nostrils the signs of the approach of death.

[20] When you saw the flesh of children burned upon the flesh of other children, severed hands upon hands, scalped heads upon heads, and corpses fallen on other corpses and when you saw the place filled with many spectators of the torturings, you did not shed tears.

[21] Neither the melodies of sirens nor the songs of swans attract the attention of their hearers as did the voices of the children in torture calling to their mother.

[22] How great and how many torments the mother then suffered as her sons were tortured on the wheel and with the hot irons!

[23] But devout reason, giving her heart a man's courage in the very midst of her emotions, strengthened her to disregard her temporal love for her children.

[24] Although she witnessed the destruction of seven children and the ingenious and various rackings, this noble mother disregarded all these because of faith in God.

[25] For as in the council chamber of her own soul she saw mighty advocates -- nature, family, parental love, and the rackings of her children --

[26] this mother held two ballots, one bearing death and the other deliverance for her children.

[27] She did not approve the deliverance which would preserve the seven sons for a short time,

[28] but as the daughter of God-fearing Abraham she remembered his fortitude.

[29] O mother of the nation, vindicator of the law and champion of religion, who carried away the prize of the contest in your heart!

[30] O more noble than males in steadfastness, and more manly than men in endurance!

[31] Just as Noah's ark, carrying the world in the universal flood, stoutly endured the waves,

[32] so you, O guardian of the law, overwhelmed from every side by the flood of your emotions and the violent winds, the torture of your sons, endured nobly and withstood the wintry storms that assail religion.

4Mac.16

[1] If, then, a woman, advanced in years and mother of seven sons, endured seeing her children tortured to death, it must be admitted that devout reason is sovereign over the emotions.

[2] Thus I have demonstrated not only that men have ruled over the emotions, but also that a woman has despised the fiercest tortures.

[3] The lions surrounding Daniel were not so savage, nor was the raging fiery furnace of Mishael so intensely hot, as was her innate parental love, inflamed as she saw her seven sons tortured in such varied ways.

[4] But the mother quenched so many and such great emotions by devout reason.

[5] Consider this also. If this woman, though a mother, had been fainthearted, she would have mourned over them and perhaps spoken as follows:

[6] "O how wretched am I and many times unhappy! After bearing seven children, I am now the mother of none!

[7] O seven childbirths all in vain, seven profitless pregnancies, fruitless nurturings and wretched nursings!

[8] In vain, my sons, I endured many birth-pangs for you, and the more grievous anxieties of your upbringing.

[9] Alas for my children, some unmarried, others married and without offspring. I shall not see your children or have the happiness of being called grandmother.

[10] Alas, I who had so many and beautiful children am a widow and alone, with many sorrows.

[11] Nor when I die, shall I have any of my sons to bury me."

[12] Yet the sacred and God-fearing mother did not wail with such a lament for any of them, nor did she dissuade any of them from dying, nor did she grieve as they were dying,

[13] but, as though having a mind like adamant and giving rebirth for immortality to the whole number of her sons, she implored them and urged them on to death for the sake of religion.

[14] O mother, soldier of God in the cause of religion, elder and woman! By steadfastness you have conquered even a tyrant, and in word and deed you have proved more powerful than a man.

[15] For when you and your sons were arrested together, you stood and watched Eleazar being tortured, and said to your sons in the Hebrew language,

[16] "My sons, noble is the contest to which you are called to bear witness for the nation. Fight zealously for our ancestral law.

[17] For it would be shameful if, while an aged man endures such agonies for the sake of religion, you young men were to be terrified by tortures.

[18] Remember that it is through God that you have had a share in the world and have enjoyed life,

[19] and therefore you ought to endure any suffering for the sake of God.

[20] For his sake also our father Abraham was zealous to sacrifice his son Isaac, the ancestor of our nation; and when Isaac saw his father's hand wielding a sword and descending upon him, he did not cower.

[21] And Daniel the righteous was thrown to the lions, and Hananiah, Azariah, and Mishael were hurled into the fiery furnace and endured it for the sake of God.

[22] You too must have the same faith in God and not be grieved.

[23] It is unreasonable for people who have religious knowledge not to withstand pain."

[24] By these words the mother of the seven encouraged and persuaded each of her sons to die rather than violate God's commandment.

[25] They knew also that those who die for the sake of God live in God, as do Abraham and Isaac and Jacob and all the patriarchs.

4Mac.17

[1] Some of the guards said that when she also was about to be seized and put to death she threw herself into the flames so that no one might touch her body.

[2] O mother, who with your seven sons nullified the violence of the tyrant, frustrated his evil designs, and showed the courage of your faith!

[3] Nobly set like a roof on the pillars of your sons, you held firm and unswerving against the earthquake of the tortures.

[4] Take courage, therefore, O holy-minded mother, maintaining firm an enduring hope in God.

[5] The moon in heaven, with the stars, does not stand so august as you, who, after lighting the way of your star-like seven sons to piety, stand in honor before God and are firmly set in heaven with them.

[6] For your children were true descendants of father Abraham.

[7] If it were possible for us to paint the history of your piety as an artist might, would not those who first beheld it have shuddered as they saw the mother of the seven children enduring their varied tortures to death for the sake of religion?

[8] Indeed it would be proper to inscribe upon their tomb these words as a reminder to the people of our nation:

[9] "Here lie buried an aged priest and an aged woman and seven sons, because of the violence of the tyrant who wished to destroy the way of life of the Hebrews.

[10] They vindicated their nation, looking to God and enduring torture even to death."

[11] Truly the contest in which they were engaged was divine,

[12] for on that day virtue gave the awards and tested them for their endurance. The prize was immortality in endless life.

[13] Eleazar was the first contestant, the mother of the seven sons entered the competition, and the brothers contended.

[14] The tyrant was the antagonist, and the world and the human race were the spectators.

[15] Reverence for God was victor and gave the crown to its own athletes.

[16] Who did not admire the athletes of the divine legislation? Who were not amazed?

[17] The tyrant himself and all his council marveled at their endurance,

[18] because of which they now stand before the divine throne and live through blessed eternity.

[19] For Moses says, "All who are consecrated are under your hands."

[20] These, then, who have been consecrated for the sake of God, are honored, not only with this honor, but also by the fact that because of them our enemies did not rule over our nation,

[21] the tyrant was punished, and the homeland purified -- they having become, as it were, a ransom for the sin of our nation.

[22] And through the blood of those devout ones and their death as an expiation, divine Providence preserved Israel that previously had been afflicted.

[23] For the tyrant Antiochus, when he saw the courage of their virtue and their endurance under the tortures, proclaimed them to his soldiers as an example for their own endurance,

[24] and this made them brave and courageous for infantry battle and siege, and he ravaged and conquered all his enemies.

4Mac.18

[1] O Israelite children, offspring of the seed of Abraham, obey this law and exercise piety in every way,

[2] knowing that devout reason is master of all emotions, not only of sufferings from within, but also of those from without.

[3] Therefore those who gave over their bodies in suffering for the sake of religion were not only admired by men, but also were deemed worthy to share in a divine inheritance.

[4] Because of them the nation gained peace, and by reviving observance of the law in the homeland they ravaged the enemy.

[5] The tyrant Antiochus was both punished on earth and is being chastised after his death. Since in no way whatever was he able to compel

the Israelites to become pagans and to abandon their ancestral customs, he left Jerusalem and marched against the Persians.

[6] The mother of seven sons expressed also these principles to her children:

[7] "I was a pure virgin and did not go outside my father's house; but I guarded the rib from which woman was made.

[8] No seducer corrupted me on a desert plain, nor did the destroyer, the deceitful serpent, defile the purity of my virginity.

[9] In the time of my maturity I remained with my husband, and when these sons had grown up their father died. A happy man was he, who lived out his life with good children, and did not have the grief of bereavement.

[10] While he was still with you, he taught you the law and the prophets.

[11] He read to you about Abel slain by Cain, and Isaac who was offered as a burnt offering, and of Joseph in prison.

[12] He told you of the zeal of Phineas, and he taught you about Hananiah, Azariah, and Mishael in the fire.

[13] He praised Daniel in the den of the lions and blessed him.

[14] He reminded you of the scripture of Isaiah, which says, `Even though you go through the fire, the flame shall not consume you.'

[15] He sang to you songs of the psalmist David, who said, `Many are the afflictions of the righteous.'

[16] He recounted to you Solomon's proverb, `There is a tree of life for those who do his will.'

[17] He confirmed the saying of Ezekiel, `Shall these dry bones live?'

[18] For he did not forget to teach you the song that Moses taught, which says,

[19] `I kill and I make alive: this is your life and the length of your days.'"

[20] O bitter was that day -- and yet not bitter -- when that bitter tyrant of the Greeks quenched fire with fire in his cruel caldrons, and in his burning rage brought those seven sons of the daughter of Abraham to the catapult and back again to more tortures,

[21] pierced the pupils of their eyes and cut out their tongues, and put them to death with various tortures.

[22] For these crimes divine justice pursued and will pursue the accursed tyrant.

[23] But the sons of Abraham with their victorious mother are gathered together into the chorus of the fathers, and have received pure and immortal souls from God,

[24] to whom be glory for ever and ever. Amen

www.ingramcontent.com/pod-product-compliance
Lightning Source LLC
Chambersburg PA
CBHW032005040426
42448CB00006B/489